AND THAT'S NOT ALL

THE STORY (AUTOBIOGRAPHY) OF JOSEPH A. LESSARD ONE OF THE FIRST PERMANENT CATHOLIC DEACONS IN AMERICA.

Edited by Ezra Small

AND THAT'S NOT ALL
Copyright © 2025 by Ezra Small

ISBN: Paperback: 979-8-218-80891-4

Printed in the United States of America

TABLE OF CONTENTS

CHAPTER 1

BORN AGAIN!

Hearing a familiar voice is not something strange. It is, however, an overwhelming experience to hear that same voice speaking in a strange new language. It's especially surprising when it was my own voice! What happened? What brought me to this moment? As I look back years later, those same memories and feelings flood back into my mind and heart. How would I have ever known what this experience would mean, and how God would change everything.

It began when an order priest from Canada took up residence in our parish rectory. His name was Father Jean Paul and we had become acquainted and were good friends. He told me about a strange and wonderful experience of the Holy Spirit happening in something called "prayer meetings." He said it was the "Baptism of the Holy Spirit." I was intrigued and he invited me to attend a prayer meeting held at a parishioner's home. I attended and as a result I had many questions. One day I was discussing this with Father Paul in the rectory kitchen. As I was leaving to head back across the church parking lot to my van, I turned my head and said: "You know if the Holy Spirit wants me, I'm His." I had no idea that Jesus would really take me up on that prayer.

I no sooner got into my van, closed the door and was about to put the key in the ignition, when I looked up over the dashboard and out the windshield. There I saw a vision. I was stunned. It was clear and translucent. I saw my mother, Cora holding a black child in her arms. She was looking upon this little one with great love and tenderness. I was held in the arms of the moment too with pure amazement and wonder. Then the tears came flooding out. At the same time, words that I could not define like sounds running together, poured out of my mouth. I got out of my van somehow and raced or staggered back to the rectory. Fr. Jean Paul was still in the kitchen, as if somehow waiting for me. I felt the mighty presence of the Holy Spirit. His overwhelming uplifting presence; and a flood of joy like the roar of many waters, break through the floodgates of my soul.

After a while, my prayer in tongues lapsed into a time of silence. I stood there motionless, as though paralyzed in amazement and perplexity. "What happened?" I asked Father Paul. "Oh," he said. "You have received the Baptism of the Holy Spirit!" It was completely unexpected. I was not prepared for this. No one had even prayed over me for the outpouring of the Spirit. Waves of praise and worship washed over me. We needed to find a more private place. So, Fr. Jean Paul and I somehow made it over to the church so I could pray there. I wanted to go before the Blessed Sacrament to give thanks to the loving and wonderful God who had so greatly blessed me. *Fr. Paul needed to get me out of the rectory kitchen and dining room.* It was a win, win decision. Together we knelt in the last pew. Once again, this beautiful gift of prayer flooded my heart with a chorus of praise like a palpable force of God's grandeur.

Although I was in glory, the world around me was the same. The pastor for some reason or other, decided to make a church visit. He came in and walked right by me. There I was, praying in tongues unabashedly, and loudly, my hands outstretched, lost in the moment. *Only the Lord knows what he must have thought.* Father Paul looked at him and just shrugged his shoulders. The Sisters of the parish came in just then to change the altar linens. I kept on praying in the Spirit. *God knows what they must have thought.* I was unaware that I had become spectacular to angels and a spectacle to everyone else. Eventually we left the church. I began to realize that although I had a deep personal experience, it had been witnessed by others. "How am I going to explain this to my wife?" I said to Fr. Paul. "Oh, just tell her in your own words what happened and how you feel." He replied.

So, I went home wondering how my wife Beatrice would handle this news? It struck me how difficult this event was to explain. Any mental rehearsal seemed woefully inadequate to describe what happened. I got home and I met Bea in the kitchen. I tried my best to tell her about it. I stammered and stuttered trying to communicate a clear message of what I had experienced. To my great joy and surprise, she exclaimed, "That's beautiful!" I remember how comforting her response felt in my heart.

Looking back, I understand now, the meaning of this, "Baptism of the Holy Spirit." It was, at the time, a confirmation of the growing closeness to Jesus Christ that was emerging in my life. Little did I know that it was also a prelude to the sufferings that would follow and the marvelous adventure that lay ahead.

The desire to share my spiritual awakening and conversion was brimming over and I wanted to tell my best friends. I wanted them to know how wonderful God's love is and how His love and presence had burst into my mind and heart. It was, in some small way, like Mary visiting her cousin Elizabeth to celebrate the Good News (Lk. 1: 39-45). I naively thought that they would be happy for me and would understand my joy and excitement. I was surprised to find that instead of rejoicing with me they not only were confounded but even painfully disapproving of my experience. They told me that it couldn't happen—least of all to me, that if something like that was possible, how was it that nothing like it had happened to them. They were good Christians too. I was not as special or religious than they were. I couldn't believe my ears. I was numb with shock. It was disappointing and painful to recognize this "Road less traveled by," (Frost, 1969) would mean leaving behind the esteem of some of my closest friends. I have grown to recognize that often people do not recognize that God's gifts are free, and gratuitous. If that means anything, it must mean that the gifts of the Holy Spirit are freely given to anyone regardless of their worthiness (1 Cor. 12: 1-29).

It was natural for me to wonder why Jesus had chosen to lavish these charismatic gifts of the Holy Spirit upon me. I could understand this blessing being poured out on monks, priests, bishops and other religious, brothers or sisters, who are living with the benefits of education, community and daily prayer and communion. I was not ordained or recognized as a theologian so I should not be able to understand what had happened to me. Yet there it was. I found myself searching through my personal history that could point to an explanation. Leafing through the archives of my mind and heart led me to one simple realization. It was an experience that happened as a matter of God's divine good pleasure. Isaiah said it this way, "Yahweh called me before I was born. From my mother's womb he pronounced my name" (Is. 49: 1-3).

I am sure of this much, when I was still nestled in my mother's womb, before I knew myself, God knew me. I was born into a loving family. My mother and father were of French-Canadian backgrounds who were far from wealthy but rich in love and who raised a family of eleven children.

We all went through and survived the Great Depression. There were many difficult days and seasons. Often, I would see my father, a carpenter by trade, toiling from morning to midnight also working our small farm. We lived humbly with simple and frugal means. I never realized as a child living in Lowell Massachusetts that our family was struggling. By today's standards, we would have been considered well below the poverty line. It seemed that everyone else was experiencing financial hardships too. What little we had was normal to us. There was, however, the solid currency of love and care in my growing up. My parents provided a loving example. I never cease praising God for the excellent loving environment that they provided where words of kindness and devotion were matched by a valued and wholesome way of life.

Looking back through the lens of my history I often reflect on how the love of God is creative. Love makes all things new. God gave me an awareness early-on to the meaning of to be born again, not just in the natural meaning of birth but to be re-created into the new life of the Holy Spirit. So it was that my father and mother carried me to the fountain of eternal life to be baptized. To be a new creation through the life of Jesus Christ. How grateful I am that my parents love was so pure and profound, so exalted and supernatural as to share it with all its Christian fullness. I have no recollection of the event, outside of the witness of my childhood community, but its reality has shaped my history and experience. I am so thankful that my parents not only brought me into and nourished me in a loving community as a child of the first Adam. Yet, they did not rest content until they had presented me into that loving community nurtured by the Holy Spirit into the heart of Jesus and the arms of God. I highlight this event because that baptism was the sacrament of initiation into the Holy Spirit and His gifts. I am reminded in scripture that charismatic gifts can precede our baptism, since God gives them as a benefit of conversion as we see in Acts:10: 44-48. However, I am thankful that even before I learned the usefulness of my tongue and language, God had planted these gifts in the depths of my soul. Praise God! It is the most profound gift of all that the Holy Trinity took up residence in my heart and the love of Christ Jesus touched the waters of my life as He does to all His children through His grace.

Looking back on my childhood through the lens of my spiritual awakening, I can see the ardent prayers of that boy who wanted desperately to serve at God's altar. I was an active and even boisterous child. Yet, stopping by the church to pray on my way back home from school produced moments of quiet reflection and calm. Often, at church my prayers would cause me to cry, which was embarrassing. I didn't realize that the Holy Spirit was consoling me back then, but I do now. My previous spiritual experience opened my heart to appreciate God's generosity. I was moved to tears and feelings of compassion when, for example, I saw the crucifix during Holy Week processions.

Although I was deeply moved by the sufferings of Jesus, I was unhappily denied the privilege of my dream to serve mass on Sunday's. as an "altar boy." I coped with this disappointment with the idea that my prayer would be answered somehow later in my life. Now I realize that I was subconsciously blessed by the belief that God had given me something more than a liturgical experience of His love, namely, an awareness of His personal presence in my heart. It is through this experience that every good gift is baptism in us and through the waters of that baptism every form of service is nurtured and produced.

God was similarly engaged in forming my future wife, Beatrice. She was born on May 7th, 1930, in Westford, Massachusetts and was a little over three years younger than I. She was the only child in her family and her parents were industrious, frugal, and active Catholics. They were generous and helped some extended family members who needed loving support. Beatrice was not a well child. Her early childhood was marred by health issues that drained her of her strength, so much so, that some doctors saw "no hope for her recovery." However, she was loved and prayed for by her parents and extended family. They prayed that her life would be sparred. They consecrated her to Jesus through the Shrine of St. Joseph in Montreal, Canada, which was founded by Brother Andre Besette (now St. Andre Besette, St Joseph's Shrine in Montreal Canada). Jesus healed her miraculously through these prayers and she was restored to good health. How strange it is that suffering can exist at the same time within the fabric of God's purposes and love's strength. She grew in love with the Lord and in service to her church. Beatrice sang in the choir, worked in the sacristy setting up for mass, and loved to worship God. She was well known in her community and through her reputation of service and caring for others, I heard about and seemed destined to meet her.

I was discharged from the Navy after World War II and upon returning home, like so many, I began praying for a spouse to share my life with. Beatrice was also praying for the same thing. It is not surprising that God's providence arranged that we should meet, become friends, soon realize that God had indeed answered our prayers; fall in love, and become engaged. I remember with great fondness, even though we had not gotten married, the look on the old banker's eyes, when we asked for a loan for fifty-five hundred dollars to build a house. As he put the papers before us to fill out, he asked me the name of my wife. I told him that we had not been married yet, but we were going to be. He was an eighty-four-year-old man. His eyes suddenly sparkled with something like a gleam of wonder or hope. "This is quite extraordinary," he observed. "We don't usually grant bank loans for a home to an engaged couple." However, our heavenly Father, who had already called us into His family, moved him to approve our loan. I started the construction on our house. With my experience in carpentry, I began working on the property we bought on weekends and at night. You know, the gleam of hope was still in that old man's eyes when he would show up every so often to see our progress at the site. He would often bring his wife with him, and they became our good friends.

Our hopes and joyful excitement increased as we closed in on the date of our wedding. It was a great celebration, but it's what happened next that certainly had the biggest influence on things to come.

Following our marriage and honeymoon, we stayed with Bea's parents while I sold lumber and worked on our new home. We soon learned that we were pregnant, normally this news is filled with joyful expectation, and we certainly felt that excitement, but it came with a huge personal cost for us. She became terribly ill. The greater part of the first four months of our marriage were spent apart while Beatrice was in a private hospital under the care of many doctors. She dwindled down to eighty-six pounds. We were praying and suffering and enduring all at the same time. God answered our prayers. After four months her health began to improve, and her strength returned. She was able to recover to such an extent that at the proper time our son Michael was born.

Life comes with many different layers of experience. Michael grew, with all the charms and spontaneous activity of a toddler, confirming the sense of Bea's recovery. With her second pregnancy though, many of the same health issues returned in the first trimester of our next child Susan.

Michael became chronically asthmatic when he was four years old. He spent lots of time in the hospital under an oxygen tent and seemed to resist all the available treatments. His health was deteriorating, and his sickness was defeating the doctor's best efforts. Finally, they threw in the towel. Their best advice was to move to a warmer and dryer climate. So, with nothing to be gained by any further medical options in Lowell Massachusetts, we decided to pull up our tent and start a trek for the city in the desert, Phoenix, Arizona in 1956. Like the fabled Phoenix in Greek mythology, we almost felt that our whole being had gone up in flames; yet we hoped for a temporal resurrection in that growing and mysterious land out-west. We hoped, if not for a complete cure for Michael, an elevation of our spirits and a general improvement in his health.

We had sung in our church choir since our courtship and we believed that singing the praises of God was praying twice, and looking back, with all those layers of life all going on simultaneously, we needed twice as much prayer to get through it. Experiencing this huge change in our life drew us closer together. Our western adventure led to spiritual growth while at the same time we continued to grow our family. Barbara, our third child, was born without the excessive difficulties of the first two. Next was another girl, Then came Richard who took the trophy for male descendants and finally our youngest daughter was born.

Michael's health began to improve as we had hoped and prayed it would, and he and Susan attended parochial school at our parish of St. Theresa Catholic Church. He served at the altar, and I praised God that my prayers for myself had been answered through him, as he became an altar boy at church which gave me a great feeling of fulfillment and joy.

Beatrice and I began to desire a prayer that would bless and unite our family as our children grew and matured. We asked God to reveal a devotional tool that we could pray together. Our request was answered on day when a priest by the name of Father Evens happened to visit our parish and preach. he spoke of the enthronement of the Sacred Heart of Jesus and the daily prayer of consecration to the Sacred Heart for families. His devotion, zeal and conviction convinced us to find out more about this and he was kind enough to provide us with more information. We had Father Evens come over to our home and we consecrated our home to the Sacred Heart of God's wonderful Son Jesus. It became part of our family's spiritual life at mealtime to offer up our petitions and praises, adding them to the prayer of consecration. It secured for our family many blessings and made us aware of the presence of God though the "domestic church." The prayer was its own blessing that united us to other segments of God's family through this bond of affection to the Heart of Jesus. Our little daughter was three years old at the time and she internalized this prayer in a profound way. One incident I remember quite clearly, because, free from my work, on a Saturday I was at home. Bea had informed me that she wanted to take our new car and go shopping. "Sure" I replied as I watched her go out the door. She wasn't gone but a few minutes when she reappeared to say that the car would not start. I said, "of course it has to start, it's a brand-new car!" She answered, "No, the battery must be dead." I shot back, "That's impossible! I said with a louder voice of frustration and disbelief. Our youngest child, sitting on the floor and nimbly tying her shoes, looked up and amazed us with her simple comment: "Peace, harmony and unselfishness," quoting from the prayer of consecration we said every day at mealtime. We were taken aback, and I picked her up and said, "that's right, peace and harmony and unselfishness." Bea and I just laughed and laughed. We had witnessed through our little child the importance of tone and the content of speech that carried the first impression of a possible conflict and argument. She had made us aware that she was listening and had a spiritual solution right at hand.

The prayer of consecration to the Sacred Heart of Jesus that we prayed goes like this:

"Dear Sacred Heart of Jesus remember that we are consecrated and belong to you. Bless and protect us all. Make our home a shrine of Your love and grace. Strengthen the bonds of affection that unites us together. Help us to bear each-others burdens in peace, harmony, and unselfishness. Keep us always near to you and to your Blessed Mother. Amen."

I am so thankful for this devotion to the Sacred Heart. It has informed my prayer life and continues to be a great spiritual source of strength for me.

Bea and I, at this time, had become more active in church. We were teaching religious education classes to children and adults. We sang in the choir, and I had begun reading, as a lector at mass studying the scriptures and preparing to read them publicly. Often, as I read the scriptural lessons, it was as if I was hearing them for the first time. The new accents and new inflections that sped directly from my throat to ears seemed to increase the vibrancy or resonance of the words. My personal rendition of the Good News illumined its interpretation back to my heart. The Epistles and Gospels had resounded, of course, for many years through the vaults of our church life and down the corridors of my childhood. Now, suddenly, it was like looking into a deep well, the more I read the deeper I peered into God's Word. I know now that it is only through the Lord's unfathomable patience and the glory of His grace, that our insights deepen the eyes of our soul, and we are gradually prepared to see the illumination of the wonder of His incomprehensible love.

I remember that on a particular Sunday, as I read the lesson to the people, the sentences were imbued with a new creative energy, which caught me by surprise. They brought tears to my eyes and deeply touched me. It was as if the words themselves had come alive. Somehow, during this public proclamation Jesus was planting a call on my life, one that would become louder and more pronounced as time went by.

A new priest had arrived from Canada to our parish. Fr. Jean Paul Regenbal from Montreal had come to work for a year and recuperate from an illness in the dry desert climate. I remember meeting him in the hallway of the rectory. We both had similar cultural backgrounds and we both spoke French. We soon became good friends. I recall showing him around Phoenix and how the city had grown and prospered. We visited the local sites, and he enjoyed sharing our common interests.

One Sunday morning he was the celebrant, and I was the lector for the readings. He noticed something new as I read the Word of God. It might have been my tone or the intention behind the inflections in my voice that caught his attention. The following week, I met with him, and he said,

"Do you know what is happening to you?" I countered back, "No," hopeful that something good was going to be uncovered. The next thing he said hardly seemed relevant, "Would you like to go to a prayer meeting?" Surprised, I asked, "What's that?" I did not know that he had received the Baptism of the Spirit a week earlier. I asked him what it was like, and he explained that a group of people meet each week to pray and seek God's Holy Spirit to be more present in their lives. "Sure, I'll go." I said,

I got the time and place from him. I asked my son Michael later that morning if he wanted to go with me and he agreed. So off we went to our first prayer meeting. The people won my esteem because they were so devoted and zealous for God's Word. However, their method of praying was so different, strange, and beautiful. I sat patiently and listened to the teachings and their testimonies about how Jesus loved us and how His Spirit moved in exciting ways. I felt a growing sensitivity to God's Word in my heart and I thought, *if this is what the Lord is calling me to, then, so be it.* My only reservation was that it must be acceptable to the universal church, particularly in the parish where I was ministering. I had noticed that the participants had come from quite different denominations and faith communities.

The following day I met with Father Paul, and he asked me how I liked the prayer meeting? "The people are very nice," I conceded. "Would you like to go again next week?" He replied. I said hastily, "I can't; I'm going to be out of town." I'm sure he saw this as a form of resistance, but my way out was true. It would be a full week before I returned to the rectory to pick up some religious materials for the class I was teaching. It happened to be another Monday and Father Paul, and I sat down to have a cup of coffee in the rectory. Father Paul looked at me and said, "Today is the day of the prayer meeting. Would you like to go?" I drew a lot of stockpiled excuses from my handy inner-self, and I said that I had just gotten back into town and had many things to do and tasks to catch up on. He did not pursue this subject further. As I was leaving the rectory, I just unburdened something deep in my heart that summed up all that needed to be said. I simply answered my own question: "If God really wants me, I'm His." Reflecting now on the love of the Holy Spirit, as I have described to you in the first pages of this book, I am reminded from the scriptures of the Holy Spirit's pure and permeating presence (Act's 2: 1-12). As I prayed in tongues on that day for the first time, without reasoning, it intuitively dawned on me that the mysterious expression on my lips almost blended with the interior impression in my spirit. They formed together one reality that I could not help but recognize as an integral way of lifting-up both soul and body in praise of God. It is an important part of my prayer life and an important charism for any person who desires to deepen their life in the Spirit.

There is little that I can add to the story of my conversion. I do not know how to give an adequate idea of this blessing, except to say that it is not exactly an uncommon experience. It was often observed among the primitive Christians, as St. Paul 's letters indicate. It is discussed in all the manuals of spiritual life. It was for my soul a launching pad for my spiritual journey. It has given me a changed new outlook on life. It has put into focus the limited perspective of the vanishing things of earth. With this experience of the God's grace has come an unparalleled ease in praising the Creator.

And that's not all!

CHAPTER II

MIRACLES AND MESSAGES

People often talk to themselves. I suppose hardly anyone is surprised to hear their own voice in an interior dialogue. In our everyday lives, we are constantly discussing matters in our heads (self-talk) that affects us. We draw from previous experience and memories, a solution to a problem, plans and goals, or a change of direction, or some desire for self-evaluation and improvement. These follow previous patterns of thought, feelings, attitudes, and intentions that overlay, and sometimes even collide with each other (Savage, 1996). Answers, revisions, rebuttals, or refinements flow from the remembrance of similar past experiences or emerge from the creativity of new ideas and new life experiences that are expressed in language. The human intellect is like a vast storeroom of tapes that provide the framework for verbalization, which includes answers, comments, objections and all other types of beliefs and information. Our knowledge, particularly what we know as memory, or understand as intelligence, is filtered through our visual, auditory, or kinesthetic senses (Savage, 1996). We continually store-up countless bits of information in orderly files of imagery which are tagged with words. If we did not, then it would be difficult to communicate or to speak intelligently, because the interior world of thought would be devoid of connection to the reality of the world outside ourselves.

The gift of praying in tongues is different from our natural understanding of language. The person does not talk to themselves but to God in words they don't understand. It is not the avenue to discuss problems or solutions. St. Teresa and St. John of the Cross point to the limitation of imagery, words, and mental concepts in contemplative prayer (St. Teresa,1980). The interior prayer of contemplation is detached from the intellectual rigors of thought since contemplation freely infused by the Holy Spirit, soars above all the natural conditions of language and the limitations of the intellect (Rom. 8: 18-27). The gift of praying in the language of the Holy Spirit acts as a doorway to enter the gift of God's love and prepares the person for a deeper contemplative experience of the presence and the love of Christ.

The enemy lives in fear and he promotes the many sins that stem from his pride. He cannot love and he cannot give real tenderness, kindness, and the genuine gifts of the Holy Spirit. He can only try to mimic them to sow seeds of division, fear, and doubt (Eph. 6:1-20). This is not the case when praying in tongues, it connects our spirit with the Holy Spirit to produce the fruit of, "love, joy, peace, patience, kindness, generosity, faithfulness, gentleness, self-control" (Gal. 5: 22-23). The purpose of this prayer is evidence of the presence of the Holy Spirit for the building-up of the church. It also brings to awareness the universality of the church which includes every language and people. It reminds us today of the apostolic church that witnessed the breath of Jesus upon them and the fiery tongues that provoked the miraculous preaching of the apostles at Pentecost (Acts, 2: 1-11).

I've had many occasions to pray over people in the hospital and elsewhere and some patients that the doctors could not diagnose the cause of their physical or emotional disease. Praying in the Spirit does not require the understanding of the person's complaint. It frees the mind from the work of formulating a prayer for healing when the cause of the illness or situation is unknown. The Spirit knows what to pray for and how to pray. It puts us in touch with the mystery and the wonder of God's grace. My experience of this gift only heightened my awareness that God is above my understanding and to trust and believe in Him. I dare say, that if the gift had no other reason other than to be a kind of "grace note" or overtone added to the interior melody of prayer and the unexpected joy and love produced by this mysterious gift. It is a wonderful cord of spiritual blessing.

I lacked an understanding of what had happened to me, at the time, but God produced three treasure- filled events to show that this unexpected experience of his grace and love was not an illusion or fantasy. Later, that very same day, November 2nd, 1969, Father Jean Paul, and a friend went to visit my father-in-law Emile Cantin in the hospital. He had been confined to bed with a severely swollen knee. There was no diagnosis to explain the symptoms. It was so painful that he could not use his leg at all. They gathered for prayer and laid hands on him praying for healing. They were not shy in lifting-up praises to God for Emile's leg to be restored. When the worship slowly quieted there was a feeling of lightness and joy that remained behind. Surprised by the experience of this gift of faith, they watched as he rose to his feet and began to walk, without pain, around the bed he was tied to by his I.V. The swelling in his knee had totally disappeared and he was discharged and sent home. While he was in the hospital, Emile had also undergone tests that showed that he had a mass on his right lung that was likely cancer. He was sent home for the thanksgiving holiday, but he and the family understood the ordeal of surgery would have to be faced in a few days.

As I reflect on this time in my early calling, I need to describe the second treasure of this story. How I was given a Word of Knowledge to share with Emile about his surgery. While he was at home before his anticipated procedure. I was privately praying for him and clearly heard a quiet voice in my heart tell me, "Don't worry. Your father-in-law will not be operated on. Go and tell him this." There it was. I was given a personal revelation; a story to tell. There would be a marvelous event a "miracle "that would gradually appear in the days that would follow. I knew, from this experience, what would happen in the future. It was not a simple desire or notion about what may or may not be God's will, but a certainty that God's plan was to heal him. The natural process of facing harsh possibilities or the emotional and physical preparation for them are wedded intimately through human knowledge and language. It was clear to me that this inner voice had communicated a Spiritual Word. It was not mine. It had not come from my mind or my unconscious-self. I was not slow to understand that this Word of Knowledge had come from God. The reason I grasped this belief was that although, I was aware that I functioned with one foot in the limited view of human material concerns, I had also been graced to have the other foot washed in the water of God's will of good pleasure. This transcendent love of the Spirit had imparted information that would become a witness to Jesus's love and glory (Jn. 17: 18-26).

The reason that I recognized this is that, although I could communicate this word through my normal speech and feelings, the information itself was far above my capacity to grasp and know, since it pertained to a future event.

Obediently I went to my father-in-law and told him, in my own simple way, "that God had told me to tell him, that he would never have to go through surgery." Of course, my words did not change the diagnosis and his treatment plan or interrupt the process for his surgery. So, in early December, he was admitted to the hospital for the procedure. Cancer treatments, in those days, were far more limited than now. It carried a darker sense of outcomes that raised the perspective of a high-risk, last-ditch effort. I expected him to be apprehensive, he had been spitting up blood and was struggling to breathe. Yet, to my surprise, he seemed unaffected by the incisive convictions of the surgeons. They had studied many x-rays and knew how to identify a carcinogenic process and knew that surgery was necessary.

I remember that morning when I left my car in the parking lot of the hospital under the bright, blue Phoenix sky, feeling clouds of uncertainty and confusion swirling in my mind. I walked slowly and deliberately, as I thought of my mother-in-law, and how she and Emile must be worried and apprehensive. It was a strange mismatch of messages, on the one hand, the Lord had told me there would be no surgery and on the other preparations were moving forward for that to happen. When I got to Emil's room, I found him clean shaven, fresh from a bath and lightly clothed in a doubly bleached linen. My heart was encouraged to find him in good spirits.

Emile had been introduced to his intensive-care nurse, and he knew the whole team, from the surgeon to the anesthetist and had been told that he would be in surgery within the hour. Yet, he was not agitated. He half-sat, half-lay there, like an executive in his easy chair. In a mood of perfect peace, he was telling me how he expected this operation to be a simple affair. Maybe he had some denial about the difficulties and complexity of this operation or had just not allowed himself to think about it too much.

I listened. I watched. I pondered and I prayed. Time does not slow down but sometimes it seems to feel that way, as the scheduled surgery approached.

A young transportation aide entered the room pushing a wheelchair. He requested that my father-in-law come with him for another X-ray.

"I was in X-ray most of yesterday. I'm sure you have the wrong patient," Emile countered.

The young man thought, *"Maybe I have,"* and he went back to the front desk to check. He returned shortly and he insisted, *"No they do want to see you in X-ray again."* So off they went with Emile being wheeled back to X-ray.

Only a few minutes later a nurse entered the room carrying a hypodermic needle to prepare my absent father-in-law for his anesthesia.

"Where is Mr. Cantin?" she asked in surprise.

"They just took him down to X-ray," I informed her, and she replied, *"Well. That is very highly irregular. It just can't be! He's due in surgery right now."*

"Well," I said with some hesitation, *"I can't help that. He went to X ray like I just said."*

The nurse left and we continued to wait for the countdown which lasted for over another hour. Finally, we heard an elevator door opening, and suddenly the doctors appeared in the room. They spoke to my mother-in-law and said that Emile would be coming up shortly. The surgeon said that,

"You can get him dressed and take him home."

Incredulously Rita half-exclaimed and half questioned, *"Has he been operated on already?"*

"No," the doctor replied unsure of his answer.

"Well, are you going to operate on him today?" His wife asked.

"No, you see there is no reason to operate. The tumor that was there is now gone. Your husband is well. I suggest that you take him home."

We were all taken again by surprise. Rita asked if Emile could go back to work, and the doctor placed no restrictions on his activities. The surgeon commented before he left the room,

"I've learned not to doubt these things. I've seen other cases; the last one was about ten years ago!"

I will never forget the joy that spread like wildfire throughout the entire floor. The news traveled fast among the staff, and it was passed around from patient family to patient. Everyone learned of the miracle that God had healed Emile.

In a little while, Emile came back up to the room. It reminded me of the Prodigal Son story in the Gospel (Lk. 15: 11-32) The difference was that there was no need for forgiveness, the Lord had healed him, and our joy was followed by a tremendous tide of gratitude for what Jesus had done. It also meant the God was not distant but the love of Jesus was present with us. It seemed like a prodigal son returning home for everyone because we were all experiencing the welcoming arms of the Father. Every one of us shared this happy reunion because all of us had come home. We did not, however, search for the fatted calf; we were too busy with getting Emile ready to go with all the discharge papers and orders. The zero hour had failed to strike, and we were ready to be on our way. My father-in-law left that room light-hearted and joyful. We walked out happier and were more blessed than when we had trudged in.

That wonderful miracle is something I will never forget. It was the second blessing of the Holy Spirit who would continue his work in other ways. It was just the beginning of a faint distant call that would grow louder in my life building up to a call to ministry.

The third treasure came through another Word of Knowledge, but this time I was called to do something. I had been baptized in the Holy Spirit for about a year. In my morning prayer-time the Lord made known to me that I should drop what I was doing and go to San Diego, which is about three hundred miles from Phoenix. At first, I tried to put this thought out of my mind, but it became stronger as the day went on. So, I went to my wife and said,

"Bea, the Lord is telling me that I should go to San Diego?"

"Well, when are you going?" Her answer was a surprise question.

"Right away." I had suddenly decided.

"I will pray for you." She quickly replied.

The Lord was asking something new of me, and I hardly knew how to respond. All I knew was that He wanted me to go and so I went. I packed a few things, said good-byes, got into my car and headed down the road on a mysterious journey. As the road ahead unwound ribbon-like before me, I asked myself what I should do when I arrived? I remembered a story I heard about St. Francis, who had been hoeing in a garden, and was asked, "What would you do right now, if you knew that you were going to die today?" The story goes that Francis replied, while he continued to work, "I would continue to hoe the garden." That made sense to me, and I decided that when I got to San Diego, I would just follow my normal pattern when I stayed there on my business trips. So, when I arrived, I checked into a motel and got myself settled. The most pressing thought was the obvious question, "Why am I here?" I opened my bible, while I sat in my room and read it hoping for an answer to my question. It was almost six in the evening, and I was still sitting there unprompted and still without a clue.

Hunger got my attention. My internal clock was ringing the dinner bell. I remembered a place on Fisherman's Warf where they served great shrimp cocktails, with tables overlooking the harbor and it was within walking distance of my motel. I enjoyed the walk near the neatly arrayed fishing and pleasure boats. It was the end to a beautiful day on the ocean and the restaurant was busy getting ready to close for the day.

I prevailed upon the waiter not to turn away his last customer, and he obliged. I happily walked outside, with ocean-fresh shrimp in hand, to find a table. A gorgeous view of the shimmering water and horizon welcomed me.

I had almost chosen a place to sit, when I noticed another man sitting at a table nearby. He saw me and invited me to join him. I went over and sat down. After some casual introductions, we began to share a little about ourselves. It turned out that we were both in the same business. He, like myself, had a family. He had just docked his sailboat after a pleasant day on the ocean. How great it was, he remarked to be able to go sailing and throw overboard all the cares and pressures of business. Turning to me he asked, *"and what brings you to San Diego?"*

I confess, I was tempted to dismiss his question with the simple word "business" and let the anchor drop there. Instead, I truthfully related that I had come without any obvious reason other than what the Lord had told me. He seemed astonished. I went on to say that I was studying to be an ordained Deacon in the Catholic Church. I related how the permanent Diaconate had been restored to the Church. He seemed pleased and confided in me that he had not been in church for a long time. The void in his spiritual life had not been satisfied with acquiring other things and by the resulting problems that flow with maintaining them. I found myself intently listening to him. I reassured him of Jesus's love and mercy. It was a wonderful gift to be in this moment of God's grace as I ministered to him.

Suddenly he exclaimed: *"Do you know what?"*

"What?" I mirrored back to him, curiously.

"You came to San Diego for me!"

The thought overwhelmed him and left him speechless. Holding his face in his hands he began to weep. It was an emotional release. To think that God would be so merciful and kind, as to send someone over three hundred miles just to invite him back into God's embrace and to return to the sacraments. We spent about an hour and a half together. During our conversation he expressed his intention to return to church and to bring his family with him. I remember how he looked as I got up to leave. He was standing there with tears still in his eyes, praising God as we said good-bye. As I turned and began to walk away, he yelled out.

"Where are you going?

I answered loudly above the sounds of the sea and the pier, "I'm going to check out of the motel."

He asked, "Are you going back to Phoenix?"

"Yes, I replied, "I have nothing else to do here."

I knew in my heart that I had completed the spiritual business that the Lord had wanted me to accomplish . My drive back to Phoenix was more like a joyous flight. I praised the Lord for this wonderful gift. You cannot imagine what a comfort and consolation it was, after my return home, for Bea and me to share with each other the marvels of God's Holy Spirit and the power of His presence. This treasure built on the other two showed us how to trust in the leading of the Holy Spirit and to be guided by His grace in ministry. We have been strengthened by many similar incidents, such as I have described. I am sure that anyone who is attentive to God's promptings and can appreciate His blessings will be strengthened as well.

St. Augustine appreciated the great miracle in the harvesting of grapes. How they had been nurtured by the pure air that had raced in from foreign lands, watered by clouds and rain, and gently warmed by a star that is more than a million times larger than the earth, and is itself a great miracle. All of which, when added to the deposits of earth's soil, stone, and its creation history, is embedded in every grape and from which we produce wine. How wonderful a gift that our offering is made of bread and wine and that the Holy Spirit uses it to produce the new creation of our redemption, the Body, and Blood of Christ (St. Agustine Sermon 272).

If the pressures of your situation and the stress you endure are overwhelming; if the uncertainty of life seems to increase your confusion and weigh down your emotions and numb your senses; I trust that sharing these treasures will give you hope as they did for me. I have come to believe that there is no difficulty or problem that cannot be healed by God's love and, His soothing power to reassure us (Romans, 8: 31-39).

It is such a blessing to be part of God's design, to participate in His plan of salvation through Jesus Christ. It is important for us to be aware of the Spirit's cues and promptings in our hearts that are carried by the wings of conscience. Despite our good intentions, we are often hard of hearing. We can be more attentive and careful to listen to the Holy Spirit's voice, with submissive and open hearts. Gradually, our spiritual ears can become sensitive and familiar with those whispered cues that so often go unheard.

It is by the grace of obedience to the Holy Spirit's will that God's purposes unfolds before our eyes, and we share in the exciting plan of His redemption.

And that's not all!

CHAPTER III

TO BE A DEACON

I t is a common experience that sickness, sufferings, difficulties and even hardships, sometimes seem to have hidden graces. They can even be a means to draw us closer to God. Praying for healing and strength, puts us in touch with our need for God's help and mercy. Our generous divine benefactor's blessings can be unexpected, and can be easily dismissed as, "good luck." Jesus invites us through His incarnation, to contemplate the great love of God in all things. experiencing His abundant and loving presence through our difficulties, joys, and sorrows. Our Heavenly Father shares with us His gifts, so that we may experience His loving presence in times of smooth sailing or in stormy weather. It is to our advantage to learn to receive the Father's favors and raise our hands up in praise no matter which way the wind blows (Mk. 6: 45-51).

The apostle Paul had a profound awareness of the relationship between giver and gift. He never tired of reminding the community that they possessed the first fruits of redemption (1 Cor. 15: 20-29) namely. eternal life in Christ and living in the Holy Spirit. They acknowledged that by receiving the gifts of the Spirit, they were witnesses to the manifest wonders produced through that same Spirit that raised Christ from the dead (Rom. 8: 11-12). This relationship between giver and gift increases, for us as for them, the intimate connection, through the gift of prayer, to God's grace and spiritual power.

In the case of Father Jean Paul and myself, the charisms of the Holy Spirit, besides making us very conscious of God's presence, also had the effect of a spiritual catalyst which is an agent that brings about change or accelerates it when chemicals are mixed. How wonderful it is when God's grace and love in the Spirit mix with our humanity and through his grace and His gifts produce marvelous things. Although the catalyst remains unchanged, its influence changes the other substances. This analogy pales in face of the experience of the activity of the Holy Spirit. Father Jean Paul and I had no doubt that the charisms of the Holy Spirit had initiated change in our lives. We felt certain that the Baptism of the Holy Spirit had strengthened and renewed us. We both knew that the ministry of Christ was powerfully present in each moment. and that the work of the Holy Spirit can change a person's life. A common cultural belief is that people rarely change, but a conversion to Jesus and the experience of the Holy Spirit changes everything and makes change possible for everyone (Acts: 2: 1-37). My conversion sparked a deep desire for unity and harmony within my spirit and a growing spiritual intention to live in faithfulness to God's Word (1 Cor. 12: 12-26). So, while Fr. Paul and I grew together as friends in this journey of spiritual growth, we both became more aware of its importance to the broader Catholic family of believers.

Fr. Paul and I decided to visit our bishop. We made an appointment with the most Reverend Edward McCarthy bishop of the Diocese of Phoenix. Our intention was to describe to him the experiences and the beautiful insights we had gained for his consideration and pastoral guidance. We were among the first Catholics to experience this renewal of the Spirit in Phoenix, and like that legendary bird rising from its ashes, we had our own resurrection story to tell. It was about how the Holy Spirt had raised us up to fly in the boundless atmosphere of the Father's love and Christ's redemption.

The bishop was very gracious when we arrived for our scheduled meeting. He welcomed us and as we sat down, he made us feel comfortable and at ease with his openness and interest. He listened very intently. He gave us plenty of time to describe what we were feeling and how the Holy Spirit was leading us. I was keenly aware of how he was genuinely and prayerfully considering and reflecting on what we were saying, trying to understand the experiences we shared. Sometimes characterizing a significant personal event can be hard to talk about because it is difficult to express in mere words. The bishop was one of those rare people that could accept a level of theological inadequacy while we tried to describe and explain what had, and what was happening to us. In some complementary ways, we were all experiencing something new. Bishop

McCarthy had only recently been consecrated our new bishop in a new diocese and we had only recently experienced the newness of being baptized in the Spirit. His parting words to us were, "If this makes better Catholics of our people, then I ask you to go and preach it with my blessing." These words of reassurance and blessing propelled us forward in the name of Jesus through the power of the Spirit.

A new time of spiritual development happened for me when Father David Geraets, a Benedictine priest came into my life. He was to lead my walk in the Spirit for the next six years as my spiritual director. He was also doing something new; establishing a Benedictine monastery in Pecos, New Mexico. We met at a retreat where he was invited to preach which I attended in Scottsdale. During the conference we met several times privately. I felt we shared a kindred spirit and that he would be immensely helpful in guiding me to a deeper walk into my spiritual calling. Soon after the retreat was over, I took a trip to Pecos to explore more deeply, with Abbot David's direction, my growing relationship with the Lord Jesus. He gave me valuable spiritual guidance. He handed me a book to take back to Phoenix with me entitled, "The Spiritual Exercise of St. Ignatius of Loyola." St. Ignatius founded the "Company of Jesus," more commonly known as the "Jesuits" I did not forget Abbot David's parting words, *"You should do these,"* meaning that I should make a retreat guided by this tried-and-true method of spiritual growth. I left with the book in my hand holding the gift that would prove to be such a blessing to me.

Our family attended St. Theresa's Catholic Church in Phoenix Arizona. A new associate priest arrived at our church his name was Fr. James Suener. He was originally from Barcelona Spain. He was sent by his order to learn English and to then go to Japan to learn Japanese. The goal was to serve the spiritual needs of immigrants from Japan that had moved to South America. He was a young Jesuit priest. The providential timing of his arrival was not lost on me. I felt confident that God had a plan in bringing Fr. James to our parish. I went to the Rectory of our church and briefly spoke with the parish secretary to make an appointment with Father James. He was there already doing some work, and he came out of his office before I had a chance to be invited in. I had the book in my hand, and I explained, *"I would like to know more about the Spiritual Exercises of St. Ignatius."* Father James and the secretary exchanged glances, and he remarked, *"I just finished saying to our secretary that I've been in this country for six weeks, and no one has asked me about Ignatius of Loyola!"*

Our first meeting was incredibly open and natural and at the same time a supernatural blessing. We talked and prayed together, every day especially to discern God's will. With Fr. James's guidance, I began to delve into the mystery and beauty of God's calling in my life. I studied and prayed, with some natural resistance, the points of what is commonly called "The Exercises," and that turned out to be a series of vitalizing, and visualizing meditations. I liked the delicate touch in this new experience of spirituality in the Jesuit tradition. I saw in it an unmistakable sign of the Lord's hand leading me into a method which, when I became proficient, I would share with others.

This period of spiritual renewal and growth was only one part of the development that was happening in my life and the life of our family. I became more focused on the ministry of the church. There was an expanding of love in our family, like a butterfly trying out its new wings. My wife Beatrice, our son Michael, and our daughters Susan and Barbara had all received the Baptism of the Spirit. We were beginning to explore ministry as we started forming new charismatic prayer groups. We began with our friends and people we knew. It was an early stage of transformation and a beautiful time of enrichment in God's grace and the blessing of His gifts. It was also an embryonic and therefore a critical stage for the Charismatic movement. People were so willing to meet, pray together, experience healing, repentance, read scripture and share their faith experiences with others. It required truly little prompting for Catholics to be baptized in the Holy Spirit. It was a time of miracles as the Spirit spread out His wings over God's people. It filled us with happiness and excitement as we witnessed His outpouring of grace and love. It increasingly attracted us to the nectar of discipleship in service to Jesus and the community.

The Lord brought another priest into our lives through my connection to the Cursillo Center his name was Fr. Frank Ambrosi. He was a tremendous servant of Jesus and although physically small he was a giant of humility and caring. He had a real affection for those who were sick and dying. His compassionate nature and love for Jesus and His people made desiring holiness infectious. I was able to accompany him in his ministry to hospitals, nursing homes, and at home visitations. We ministered together to those who were suffering. Both of us realized that we were really a trio as we witnessed the signs and wonders worked by the Lord because Jesus was so present. It was through Fr. Ambrosi and our ministry together that I learned how to minister to the sick, and to provide spiritual comfort in their pain or hardship. They so desperately needed someone to pray with them because they were too ill to even pray for themselves. Mingled with the harsh reality of caring for those in pain and affliction was the experience of being blessed by the Lord's presence that tethered us to the love that He has for us and every person.

While I engaged in the ministry of visitation, I continued with the development of my prayer life through the Spiritual Exercises of St. Ignatius. I met with Fr. James every day for ninety days while I completed the Exercises and continued my work and ministry with Fr. Ambrosi. Then I arrived at the chapter of the Exercises where the person is faced with a choice (called an election). It was at this point that Jesus bestowed upon me one of His richest blessings (Loyola, 1999). It happened in the early part of July 1970. Perhaps it was because several priests had previously urged me to become a Deacon, that I remember that time so clearly. It was on July 8th that I decided to enter the new Deacon training program and to make my personal choice to follow the Lord into a new and wonderful calling of service to His people. It dawned on me, at that moment, that all I had gone through, the changes in my life, and our spiritual growth and family experiences, had been about this choice, this calling. The pieces suddenly fell into place with a great aha, "epiphany" moment of excitement and joy.

I became anxious to return home and tell this good news to my family. No better time or place, I thought, than at dinner tonight. Dinner time came and all the family was present, Michael who was a sophomore at Arizona State University studying architecture, and all the other children who were enjoying Michael's time at home. I spoke up above all the chatter to inform the family that I had an announcement to make. In the interval of growing silence that followed, we heard Michael say that he also had an announcement of some good news to make. *"You are the eldest son."* I said good humoredly, *"What do you want to tell everyone!"* Michael spoke up and slowly said, *"I decided today to consecrate my life to Jesus and become a priest."* As soon as we heard his words, feelings of joy reverberated around the table. After the excitement quieted down, I announced my intention to enter the permanent Deacon program that was being developed by the Diocese. We had never discussed our separate calls before. This surprise filled everyone with happiness. This experience has not failed to sustain us in times of difficulties and in times of celebration. All this took place in the summer of 1970 and at the same time, our home charismatic prayer-meetings continued to grow. As many as forty people would show up on a Saturday evening. Charismatic prayer groups began to be replicated by others who had experience the baptism of the Holy Spirit and it grew into a movement that continues to bless the church.

In the fall, the diocese of Phoenix began its training classes for candidates for the diaconate. I met for the first time with others who felt a calling to ministry. We, perspective deacons, compared notes and rejoiced with one another over this new, almost novel, outpouring of divine love. It was as if, the Holy Spirit was skipping over the centuries, calling back married men, in ordained service to the Catholic community of faith. We were so happy that the Second Vatican Council and the American bishops had wisely put into motion the restoration of the permanent diaconate. We knew that there were always deacons going back to Stephen (Acts 7: 1-60). Over the centuries it had come to be viewed as a temporary state, as a mere steppingstone to the priesthood. Now, it can be chosen as a permanent calling to ministry along with the vocation of marriage since both are holy sacraments and signs of God's love and presence in the world. The church was wise to recognize the compatibility between the love of a married couple and the fidelity of a calling to ordained service to the bride of Christ, the church. What would the Catholic church do without the family? It produces its future generations of believers, clergy, religious communities, and ministries. What would the family be without the church? It nurtures our spiritual life. It sustains us through the Word and in the Sacraments. It teaches and guides us into a life of holiness. In marriage, the author of everything extends His creative love, ever tending toward the fulfillment of life. It brings forth its fruit to the font of the "new creation" Jesus our Lord and Savior. Through Christ and in union with Him we are brothers and sisters of the one eternal Father's family (Eph. 4: 1-6).

Going back to my childhood desire to serve mass at the altar and my devotion to the Blessed Sacrament, I had no idea that God's calling was planted in these early longings and prayers. The permanent diaconate was unthinkable in those days. God knew, however, that He would answer my prayer and bring me into the service of His people. I would never outgrow the joy of this calling. It has only deepened with the passage of time. This tiny seed that was sown through my childhood tears, has grown into a calling of ministry to God's people (Matt. 13: 31-33). I praise God for this wonderful and blessed gift.

September 1970 was the start-up for the permanent diaconate program in the Diocese of Phoenix. There were considerable hurdles to be overcome and questions to be answered in building something from scratch. For example, what should be taught? Since this was so new, there was no handbook or detailed description of the role and ministry of married deacons. There was no timeline for training or instructional materials. How could our director put together a multi-faceted curriculum in the absence of a history, past practices, and material references?

Father William O'Brian was appointed by bishop McCarthy to be the first director of the training and education program. He was well suited for the task. He was a Carmelite priest and a canon lawyer. It would be his job to create and initiate a two-year process of equipping those moving into and through diaconate formation. The first class consisted of thirteen candidates. We quickly established a mutual bond of fellowship between us, since in many ways, both students and teacher were tossed into the same boat trying to navigate the waters of ecclesial uncertainty.

God's divine providence guided the education and formation process. Every time there was a need for a special teacher or expert in theology and pastoral care, that very person would step off the plane and come to share their time and expertise. The Father's guidance was evident in this process, and it directed our class from the beginning of our training. We felt blessed and encouraged as we explored the wonder of reclaiming and making new this work of the Holy Spirit (Acts, 6:1-7). Our natural understanding was insufficient to the task, yet our excitement did not diminish because the path was difficult and uncertain. It was enough that the Holy Spirit was leading us forward to a goal of immense value (Phil. 3: 12-16). The same Spirit that binds the Father and the Son in the Holy Trinity was also anointing us with a clear appreciation of the importance of our calling. I recognized this testimony and blessing in my experience, in my brother candidates, their families and my family. We shared this same journey of faith. It was like the formation of frost on a windowpane. The ice crystals begin to take shape slowly, from the combination of moisture in the air and cold temperature to create a form that is symmetric and beautiful. The growing evidence of God's provision, in those years of training, made real for me the importance of relying on the Father's care, kindness and love.

My family and I began to experience a deeper dependance on Jesus for the blessings of each day. The scriptures of the lilies of the field that are so beautiful, or the birds that wing their way over the earth that are cared for and fed, slowly became a pattern of my life (Mt. 6:25, Lk. 12:22). There was a growing awareness, for Bea and me through incidents and reflection, by setting our hearts on Jesus was leading us into a way of life based on Divine Providence.

In the latter part of 1970, good friends and even casual acquaintances began to give us money to care for the poor. They understood, more than I did, that I was being trained to serve those in need. At first, our benefactors gave small amounts. Gradually the donations increased through the remaining two years of my training. Through the gifts (alms) that I received and passed on to the needy, I was blessed to witness the charity of our brothers and sisters in Christ. It grew into a deeper spiritual sensitivity for the suffering of the sick and those who needed caring, compassion and physical assistance. I prayed that the Holy Spirit would guide me to those persons who needed help and support. Repeatedly, God figuratively supplied, multiplying the bread and fish through our ministry (Jn. 6 :1-15). While those who gave generously learned to share, I was learning the lessons of caring. I am sure this was a fundamental way in which the Holy Spirit was teaching us how to trust in God's generosity and provision.

As our families' devotion to the Lord increased, so did Bea's and my appreciation and love for the Holy Family. We learned to approach supernatural things more spontaneously and trustfully through a growing relationship with the Blessed Mother. I had first been introduced to her by my mother. When I was sixteen years of age, I fell from a horse and injured my back. I could not cross my legs without pain, even sitting was painful. This happened in Massachusetts and the doctors did what they could for my injury, but I did not get any relief. The accident happened in 1942 during World War II. I was planning on serving my country by joining the Navy and becoming an aircraft gunner. However, my injury was a major obstacle. I was beginning to lose hope. The doctors tried various treatments that all failed to make any improvement in my condition. I knew that under my present situation I would not pass the physical. One day my loving mother Cora, said to me, *"Let's make a novena to our Blessed Mother. Let's ask her to intercede for us, that you might be healed."* I gratefully accepted her offer and together we began the novena. To my astonishment and wonder, on the ninth day I found myself totally healed. The prayer of mother and son was answered. I was never troubled with the affliction again. Thereafter, on my seventeenth birthday I enlisted in the U.S. Navy, passed all the physicals, and became the Naval Aviator I so earnestly longed to be. In all my flights during the four years of my military service, I carried and prayed the rosary to our Lady.

Bea and I had six wonderful children, and our growing family included our deepening commitment to our Catholic church community. We entrusted our ministry of caring to Mary, seeking her maternal guidance and love. She did not keep us waiting for very long. Bea and I had come to realize that Mary's consent, (fiat) mirrored the themes of our own "yes" to the Holy Spirit (Lk. 1 : 20-37). We shared a growing spiritual inspiration that God was calling us to a new way of life. The unity we shared together in prayer confirmed the steps we were about to take for our future. It came from a persistent desire and invitation to trust God more concretely and with a greater attachment to the safety of His divine provision. It meant laying aside my commercial involvements (I was president of the Wholesale Millwork Company and the Aztec Door Company, which I had formed with two other partners nine years before). Bea and I made the decision to sell our portion of the companies and that just took four days. The materialistic burden I had been carrying was lifted from my shoulders. I felt liberated, free to trust that taking the Road Less Traveled (Frost, 1968) was a matter of holy obedience, commitment, and trust in God's divine providence. He would supply our needs. This was not an escape route away from responsibilities, or an arrogant putting God to the test, although for some it may seem that way, rather it was a willing acceptance of a profound invitation into service and mission (Matt. 4: 1-11).

Bea and I had our decision confirmed when some friends invited us to go with them to Rome for the beatification of Father Maximilian Kolby. We knew nothing about his story, but the opportunity to visit this city was exciting and we decided to join them. I had recently sold my companies, so we had the resources to go on the trip. What surprised us was that there were no reservations available on the flight with our friends. I felt a confidence that we were going to travel on that plane, and we set our sights in prayer, asking Jesus to make a way for us. Our prayers were rewarded, and two seats somehow became available, and off we went to Rome!

I will pass over the ocean of details that describe all the sights and experiences that have filled our memory with joy and wonder. Highlighting the exquisite art of Michelangelo's Pieta in fluid marble, or the Sistine Chapel that have been described so often by others. We enjoyed our visit to the Italian countryside, its cities, especially Florence, and Venice.

There were two major blessings that spiritually touched us and summed-up and distilled the experiences we had, including all the wonders of artistic creativity and the rich history and tradition of the Vatican. The beatification of Father Maximillian Kolby was the first event that touched our souls. 10,000 people from Poland, which was still behind the iron curtain at the time, were allowed to attend the beatification. They were allowed to carry only $5.00 with them by the government. The liturgy of beatification with the priests and pilgrims was very holy and left a profound impression in our hearts. What a magnificent experience to hear this vast throng singing hymns that echoed the celebration of this Polish priest's witness, martyrdom, and life. We will never forget the homily of Pope Paul VI when he spoke of the beloved Franciscan father who was a prisoner in World War II by the Nazi's and who was martyred within the time of our generation. He pointed out the heroism and sanctity manifested in his willing sacrifice of his life in exchange for the life of another prisoner. Out of all the horrors and destruction and carnage of the war, his testimony to the victory of Jesus Christ goes out to the world as a sign of Christ's redemptive love. The Pope pointed out Fr. Kolbie's faithfulness and devotion to Jesus and the to the Immaculate Heart of Mary. The description of his character and his love for God's people impressed upon us the importance of the virtue of humility that was so apparent in his life (Jn. 15: 1-27).

Two days later we attended the Pope's general audience. We found ourselves in this modern and immense hall together with many other people. The joyous experience of so many believers, tourists, pilgrims, fraternities, and representatives of religious and international organizations was breathtaking. We had the added blessing of sitting near the aisle our Holy Father took as he was escorted, right by us, to the speakers platform. This topped off the unforgettable pilgrimage that Bea and I shared and have recalled and celebrated throughout our lives and later birthed into our international ministry.

Returning to the States, meant leaving the mountain-top experience of Italy behind and settling back in the Arizona desert with no employment and a needy family to care for along with the needs of the poor. We made the best of what we had but that was slowly being swallowed up through the course of events and by those who needed ministry. I saw the Lord's leading though it all. We were being taught to rely on Him daily for our support through prayer and believing in His Word (Eph. 1: 7-14).

The scriptures reveal that Jesus invites us to share in the characteristics of His life by sharing in His cross and to shoulder it willingly (Lk. 9: 23). As we do, the cross loses a great deal of its weight. It ceases to be a burden (Mt. 11:

28-30). In a light and gentle manner Jesus was giving us a taste of the life of divine providence.

When we returned from Rome, I investigated various business opportunities for development and management of new products. All my efforts produced nothing. They only accomplished the final draining away of our savings. The family's financial situation was desperate. One day I had to face the fact that I was down to my last twenty-dollar bill. It sets the stage for the second blessing that I mentioned. I was out of town and decided to visit a nearby church. I prayed there alone before the Blessed Sacrament for a brief time. Another man came in and knelt nearby. While I was praying, I heard the Lord say, very clearly, *"Give him your twenty dollars."* I replied, *"But I will have no lunch."* The voice insisted, *"Give him the twenty dollars."* So, I took the legal tender of all debts, public and private from my wallet, and folding it neatly, I walked over to the man and slipped it into his shirt pocket. I remarked simply, *"I wish I had more, but that is all I have."* I know that he had no idea of how true that was. He smiled and his face brightened up as he confided, *"I came to pray for food for my family."* Joyfully he praised God, thanked me, and left.

Now it was my turn. I prayed that Jesus through His resurrection and His care for the world would likewise provide for me now and in our future ministry to His Body. Within a half hour another man entered the church. I felt a spiritual awareness of this man's kindness. I never expected what was about to happen. He came up to me and gently handed me, you guessed it, a stack of the same legal tender of the same denomination one hundred twenty-dollar bills in all. The Sacred Scriptures speak of the "hundred-fold blessing" (Mk. 10: 30) and here it was. May the Lord be praised for His generosity and His surprising gifts.

And that's not all!

CHAPTER IV

DIVINE PROVIDENCE

I t would be inappropriate to suppose that God only intervenes and provides just when there is a financial need. Trusting in Divine providence does not identify God as a kind of all-knowing bank executive who looks far into the future and knows the commercial outcomes of a project, or who calculates the day-by-day growth of investments by a mere glace at a magical portfolio. God does not safeguard and assure the success of His business ventures by comparing past profits with future prospects. It is His love that is carries God's transcendence, and omni-presence. His love comprehends the tiniest particle of matter swirling in space and every physical law of the universe that He continues to set in place. His love is in every infinite detail making life possible while providing everything for its existence (Matt. 17: 26-31). Trusting in Divine providence is, in my opinion, a recognition of God's comprehensive design in loving you and me, the world, and its people.

I remember something that happened around the same time that bears out the importance of trusting in the love of Jesus in the Spirit. One night I received a phone call from my friend and mentor Fr. Ambrosi. He needed a ride to the hospital to visit a patient. Father had a great ministry to the sick and he was often called by the hospital staff and patients families to anoint the ill and dying. When I arrived in my car to pick him up, he told me that a certain lady had asked to be anointed. *"I have only a name and a room number at the hospital,"* He said. *"The woman who called gave me a room number, 220 and couldn't give more details."* The hospital is huge and has many different wings with many patients waiting for different kinds of tests moving back and forth. This was before computers, and finding a patient relied on more information than we had. When we arrived, we headed in a general direction toward the middle of the hospital looking for a patient with only a name and room number. We had no idea where the patient was, so we prayed in the Holy Spirit for guidance. As we stood there in prayer a nurse suddenly came up from nowhere and asked, *"Are you here to see my patient in room 220?"* Fr. Ambrosi replied, *"yes."* The nurse led us into the room. Where we prayed for the woman and Father Anointed her. The dear lady was called to heaven the next day. This is just one small instance of how the Lord validates faithfulness. Fr Ambrosi and I were blessed in the joy of having have been permitted by the Holy Spirit to be led to do God's will. Many things could have happened to derail this divine appointment, a broken elevator, a flat tire, or accident, going to the wrong floor, or an impatient late-night nurse, or our patient could have been moved to a different floor or even died. Yet here we had a providential series of events each leading our way step-by-step to minister and pray for this patient in her time of spiritual need.

Many could question whether this was a supernatural incident or just a natural coincidence? To me, life is like a home built on the dividing line between a county or state. Crossing over from one district to another because of their proximity to each other would be a common experience. It would be difficult, at times, to tell which territory that I was in, and sometimes I might even have my feet in both. Love is the key boundary that defines God's territory and that has no limitations (Lk. 1:37: Matt. 19: 26). The Holy Spirit's Divine nature orders all things and provides the pattern of the Father's love throughout all creation. There are no accidents because outside of God's intention nothing exists. The Holy Spirit's creative union with the Father and the Son includes all of nature from the tiniest seed to plants, insects, animals and to us revealing His presence in all things (Eph 1: 3-14).

Four friends of mine and I decided to take a day and thank the Lord for all the blessings we had received in serving the people of God. We contacted Father David, who by now was my spiritual director, and asked him if he would give us a day of retreat at the Nada Ranch near Sedona, Arizona; he agreed, and we met there. Driving to the ranch, at that time, was a bit of an adventure since it meant following the upsurging slopes of the red-clay desert through an unfamiliar landscape. Once there, we followed a cement stairway leading down into a quaint little chapel. It might have also been suitable as a wine cellar. It was dimly lit by small stained-glass windows that cast little shafts of light along the solid gray walls. This underground chamber was quiet and still. We settled in the chairs, and we began to pray before the tabernacle illuminated by a small vigil light burning beside the stairway.

I recall a quotation from the poem from The Spiritual Canticle of St. John of the Cross (Collection, 1991)

> "O desert resort deserted
> > planted by the hand of the beloved—
> Tell me,
> > did you see Him passing haste fully,
> > spilling nature's graces wastefully,
> > except they image Him so tastefully?
> Ah, let me keep vigil for My beloved,
> > and with a sentinel's watchful attitude
> > silently pace the citadel's solitude,
> > trampling the thistles and thorns of solicitude,
> alert on contemplation's altitude" (vs: 4, 5, and 35).

I felt the blessing of God's simplicity and peace begin to wash over me as I began to say the Jesus prayer, *"Lord Jesus Christ have mercy on me a sinner"* God's grace burned into my heart. As I worshiped. What happened still remains a wonderful mystery to me. We had been praying silently for three hours and somehow the time flew bye. I suddenly felt myself being carried away "transported" only God knows where, and in that place, I saw, clearly inscribed, on what appeared to be a piece of frosted glass, these words: *"The Jesus Prayer."* It was brilliantly etched and clearly drawn. These words were holy and glorious and full of light.

When I slowly came back to myself from this mystical country, I was prompted by the Lord Jesus with these words: *"Say this prayer out loud three times."* I felt a natural reluctance to speak out and disturb the others with me. I somehow was able to summon enough strength to break the quiet stillness and I spoke and slowly repeated three times, *"Lord Jesus Christ have mercy on me a sinner."* I had hardly finished this petition, when all five of us found ourselves lying prostrate on the floor of the chapel. Each one of us became aware of the unexpected power of God's love that had come over us. We even felt powerless to stand up. It was only after some minutes had past that we were able to get to our feet. Father David interpreted what had happened after we had left the chapel. He said, *"You entered into contemplation and the Lord taught you this prayer."*

I did not know that *"The Jesus Prayer"* was one of the oldest forms of prayer of the Christian faith. It comes from the biblical texts of the ten lepers who pleaded with Jesus from some distance saying: "Jesus, Master have mercy on us (Lk. 17:12) and the plea of the two blind men who said, *"Take pity on us, Son of David"* (Matt. 9:27). This prayer, I later learned, was used, and passed down by pilgrims in the Eastern Orthodox Church as an important tool of prayer and devotion and can be found in the book, *"The Way of the Pilgrim."* I have received this prayer as my own and it is deeply rooted in my heart. I employ its benefits by repeating it throughout the day. This prayer even continues when I am asleep because I have often awakened with it on my lips. I have discovered that through the *"Jesus Prayer"* combined with repetition and God's grace to say it, we can celebrate the love of Jesus and worship Him with every breath (Pokrovsky, 2001).

St. Paul in Ephesians 7: 18, encourages us to pray all the time. He does not exhort us to do the impossible. instead, he urges us to remain in the presence of the Lord Jesus. We have many tools at our disposal, praying in the Spirit, thanking Jesus, reading scripture, meditating on the Word, being in communion with our brothers and sisters (the Body of Christ) with prayer and supplication, and by witnessing to the power of His name, for intercession, blessing and mercy (Col. 4:1-6; Phil. 2: 8-11;1 Cor. 12: 4-11; Phil. 4: 4-7; Rom. 12: 1-3, 4-6). It was through this prayer that the Holy Spirit introduced Beatrice, our family and I to the life of Divine Providence. I praise God for having shown me how to lift up my soul in a way that is so acceptable to Him.

It is not difficult to understand why our petitions are intimately involved with the gifts of God's providential care and love. The ten lepers, though keeping their distance from Jesus, as was required by the law, had no greater desire than to be cured of the disease that made them outcasts from society. God's grace covered the distance that the law had imposed (Rom. 6: 14). Trustfully, they prayed, and we can scarcely imagine their excitement and joy, as they saw their skin exchanging its dying discolor with the blush of health. The importance of on-going prayer is contrasted by the disappointment of Jesus when only one leper returned with a prayer of thanksgiving (Lk. 17: 15-19). Prayer is a part of Divine Providence because trusting petitions are in the center of God's care-filled provision. Sometimes we know what someone needs, but until that person acknowledges it, the acquiring of it will be unimportant. God sees and knows our needs but until we do, there may not be a recognition of their significance or value. God's grace is wrapped-up in our requests. Fulfillment encompasses the prayer of petition. From the Creator of all things comes the power to desire and to obtain, to will and to achieve. (Matt. 7: 7-12).

How the Lord Jesus moves among His people in compassion and providence was brought home to me late in 1970. My wife's cousin was visiting us, and she requested our prayer for her son-in-law living in Massachusetts. She was deeply concerned about this relative, who had suffered the loss of sight in one eye when it was pierced by a flying sliver of steel as he was working, one wintery morning, as he tried with a hammer to free his bulldozer's frozen axel.

In keeping with our practice of praying for these intentions, we gathered a small group together to pray for the son-in-law three thousand miles away. She stood in for him as we prayed over her as a spiritual proxy for his healing. Little did we know how quickly our prayers would be answered. At that very hour of our prayer, he received his sight, and he was healed. I cannot help but be reminded of the nobleman or the court official who with strong faith asked to cure his boy, "Go home," Jesus told him, "Your son will live." On the return journey he was met by his servants with the news that the boy was well. He inquired when it was that his son began to recover, and they told him at the seventh hour. He realized that this was the exact time when Jesus told him "Your him your son will live."(Jn, 4: 4-7).

I had received a letter about the healing from Bea's cousin and a few weeks later we were blessed to visit my family in Massachusetts. We were invited to visit by Bea's cousin and come and witness for ourselves the wonderful healing that had happened. That evening we met the son-in-law, together with a number of town folk who Bea and I knew very well. Red, the man with the once splintered eye, told us how he can clearly see. However, the doctor upon examination had told him that he could not see because the eye was as damaged as before. Yet here he was seeing perfectly out of that eye. There was no medical explanation possible. There was only one drawback; he still suffered severe headaches, and even while we were visiting, his head hurt so badly that he could hardly stand it. So, I asked the little group of friends who were there to join Bea and I in prayer and to ask God to completely heal our brother in Christ. We gathered around him and laid hands on him and as we prayed the pain totally disappeared. Red wept with the consolation and relief of from the pain he suffered. He expressed sincere gratitude to Jesus for being so present among His people and so mindful of his need for more healing (Mk. 8: -25). Red is still able to see without pain in both eyes to this present day.

Sharing our mutual joys and common concerns and how God was working in our lives not only included our family story but our new prayer community. As the Catholic Charismatic movement in the church expanded, so did my involvement in prayer meetings throughout the week. These evening meetings included prayer, scriptural instruction, and witnessing to the kingdom of God and the movement of the Holy Spirit leading us into a deeper walk with Jesus. Prayer meetings often meant long hours, which was the case of our trip to Massachusetts. On the last day there I wondered in prayer *"How was it that , although the little prayer meeting had seen signs and wonders, besides having the Good New preached to them , no one had asked to be prayed over for the Baptism in the Holy Spirit?"* I decided to leave that question with the Lord while I thanked and praised Him for all that we had witnessed during the week.

The next morning the phone rang as we were packing our things and preparing for the trip to the airport and to Phoenix. A member of our prayer meeting called to tell me some exciting news. He had attended mass that morning and on the door of his parish church was an announcement. It said that a Jesuit priest from Boston was to speak in the parish hall that evening. He would be explaining the gift of the Charismatic Movement in the Catholic Church. Our friend's enthusiasm and joy was a wonderful sign of blessing. We celebrated how the Spirit had laid the groundwork through our ministry and that God had prepared and provided for His people. A prayer group was formed in that town, and later it joined with a group located at a Catholic seminary about twenty miles away. I have heard that as many as three or four hundred believers gather to praise and worship the Lord in spirit and truth (Jn. 4: 24). The Scriptures remind us how little it matters *whether we, ourselves, sow the seed or enrich the soil, till the furrows, or uproot the weeds, as Paul says: "I did the planting; the watering Apollos did; But God made the plants grow"* (1 Cor. 3: 6). It is not about the planter or the waterer but about the Lord Jesus who makes things new and grow.

One of the things I was doing, at that time, was teaching a religious education class in a Phoenix Catholic High School. One day I had a providential meeting with a Jesuit priest who also taught there. We had several conversations about the Spiritual Exercises of St. Ignatius, which I had completed. During one of our discussions, he caught me off guard by remarking, *"You should conduct the Spiritual Exercises for others."* Really, I had never even considered giving this type of retreat. So, we prayed together with a view of being open to the direction of the Holy Spirit and to place it in God's hands. If it were His will, He would make it known to me.

Several Sundays later, out of the blue, two priests came to ask me if I would lead them on a retreat in the Ignatian manner? I was still somewhat reluctant, because of my lack of experience and limited background. We decided to pray together to seek the Holy Spirits guidance. We came to an agreement that I would be willing to take on this task, but only one priest at a time. The Exercises, that normally take thirty days, can be extended for ninety days, which includes prayer, meditation, and spiritual direction. They can be adapted not to hinder working people from maintaining their responsibilities while on a personal retreat (Loyola, 1999).

I was able to direct retreats for other priests, deacons, religious sisters, and laymen. While I was conducting a retreat for a religious sister, I began to wonder how this kind of retreat might be adapted for people in the parish. The Holy Spirit led me to structure them in a seminar format in each of two weekends for nine months. These retreats were open to those who wanted to participate. I directed several retreats with this method. They blessed those who attended and gave me a deeper love for God and a more solid trust in the guidance of the Holy Spirit.

The nature of God's design, in creating us and the universe, reveals the Holy Trinity's generous Divine Providence. It pours out creation through the unity of the Father the Son and the Holy Spirit's perfect love. It is that love that stirred chaos from darkness to light and confected the soup of matter into order and orchestrated its physical properties (Gen. 1:1-31; Job; 38: 1-40). This leads us to God's promises in the Old Testament and their fulfillment by His Son Jesus in the New Testament (Matt. 5:17). We cannot produce good fruit for the Kingdom of God, unless we are conscious and trusting in God's Divine Providence, since every good act comes from the inspiration of the Holy Spirit (2 Cor. 3: 17-18). Eventually, I must come to the realization that if there is any possibility of success in achieving anything worthwhile for the Kingdom of God, it resides in the Lord's provident love and care. There is a more excellent way that St. Paul distills and describes for us, faith, hope, and love (1 Cor. 13: 1-13). Although my natural gifts may pass away, faithful, hopeful, and loving submission to Divine Providence will win for me the greatest blessings of God's unfailing care. It is a joy to wait in faith and experience how the Blessed Trinity provides for us.

"By waiting and by remaining quiet you will be rescued; in tranquil confidence is your strength. For the Lord is waiting to show you, His favor; He longs to rise and take pity on you." (Is. 30: 16-18).

I have found this to be true in my life. Countless experiences in my spiritual journey confirm and witness to God's Divine Providence.

And that's not all!

CHAPTER V

THE MINISTRY

My first class of studies for the Diaconate in the Diocese of Phoenix began in September 1970. There were ten who came together, filled with enthusiasm at the prospect of becoming Deacons. I was a bit anxious about what would be expected in the months ahead. I remember how, a few weeks before, the other candidates and I had gone and met with our new Bishop Edward A. McCarthy. He had recently been appointed by the Pope to establish a new Diocese located in Phoenix. His office and apartment were temporarily situated at St. Joseph's hospital. We had hardly expected that Divine Providence would intervene so soon.

It became clear to us, once our classes began, that the service and vocation of a Deacon required more than a superficial knowledge of the liturgy and the scriptures. We found these classes to be difficult and demanding but also exhilarating and inspirational. We knew that the requirements of our education and training would impact our social lives. I felt blessed, as did my family, by a growing awareness of God's providential care for us. This process of spiritual preparation only intensified my appetite for the bread of God's Word (Jn. 6: 35). Carving out a theology of diaconal ministry was a unique calling in itself. This was a new thing to us, but in fact, it was the reclaiming of an ancient root of ordained service and ministry described in Acts and now extended to us (Acts 6: 1-7). We were the first class in Arizona. All of us, candidates, teachers, and trainers, were an important part of establishing and developing the curriculum that other dioceses would use as a template.

I was ordained May 29th, 1972, after two years of preparation. It was a thrilling and wonderful time of grace. I felt so grateful to Jesus for this sign and gift of ordination and His calling to serve the people of God. We approached the order of Deacon by taking steps commonly called, in those days, the Minor Orders. I remember this distinctly because we were the first and last class to receive them. Each step, Porter, Acolyte, Lector and all the others, raised my appreciation for the journey of faith that my family and I were undertaking.

I wish that I could adequately describe the Liturgy of Ordination as clearly as I felt it in my heart. The ten of us knew that we were placing our lives face down, prostrate at the feet of our Bishop and God's people. It was a powerful symbol of our willingness to be servants of the Bridegroom and His bride the church (Rev. 21: 1-6). It was thrilling to hear the prayers of the community with the Litany of the Saints echoing off the spacious walls of the cathedral. It was like a choir of angels surrounding us. Along with these prayers, the words of the Bishop also were resounding in my in my heart as he said, while I placed my hand on the bible and he said, *"Believe what you read, teach what you believe, and live what you teach"*(Catholic Rite of Ordination, 1969, p. 204). I affirmed that the daily reading and hearing of God's Word is an experience of faith that is to be shared with others. It's teaching is confirmed by the convincing testimony of the works and wonders of the Father the Son, and the Holy Spirit (1 Jn, 1: 1-4). The ordination rite eloquently pushed forward the core ideals and invitation to become through God's grace and mercy a sign of the communion of Jesus within us (Matt. 1: 23).

Bishop McCarthy did not assign us a parish to serve during the ensuing year. I think, looking back, that his decision was very wise. We would be assigned after a year of reflection and prayer. It gave us time to clarify and strengthen our ministry and to be led by the Holy Spirit. It was a wonderful gift to the church celebrating, not just ordination, but the unity of the sacramental ministry of deacon, priest, and bishop. This was clearly articulated by St. Ignatius of Antioch when wrote to the deacons in the 2nd century AD,

"It is necessary, then, and this to be sure, is your practice—that you never do anything without your bishop. But more than this, you should be subject to the priests also, representing, as they do, the apostles of Jesus Christ, our hope, in whom we are expecting to have eternal life. It is necessary, furthermore, that the deacons,

the dispensers of the mysteries of Jesus Christ, should in every way have the approval of everyone, for they are not merely dispensers of food and drink, but ministers of the church of God" (Ig. Trall 2-3; Roer, 2012).

"In like manner, let all respect the deacons as representing Jesus Christ; respect the bishop as a type of Father; and respect the priests as God's high council and as the Apostolic College." These words of St. Ignatius testify to the unity of Holy Orders in the early church (Ig. Trall. 3:1; Roer, 2012).

The ministry and order of Deacon is very ancient. It goes back to the early church (Acts, 6: 1-7). Among the earliest Christian disciples, as among the Jews, there were some who spoke Hebrew and others who were fluent in Greek. United in faith and love, they nevertheless encountered some causes for disagreement. The Greeks complained that their widows were being slighted in the distribution of food. The apostles called a full meeting of the disciples, in which this problem was pointed out and discussed. The apostles understood their primary calling as evangelical (preaching) and liturgical (leading worship). The equal distribution of food should be left to others. So, the apostles suggested that the community select from their members seven men who were gifted, not only with wisdom and the Holy Spirit, but also with good reputations in the church (Acts, 6: 3) to be assigned to this task. Their solution pleased everyone. The delegation of the ministry of service is not commonplace or insignificant. It was an important assignment because it flows out of the ministry of pastoral care for the community of faith. It included, therefore, a context of service to the Body of Christ and to the Word of God (James, 2: 14-26). However, as we shall see, it was an important assignment and "ordination" to official hierarchical functions. The text in Acts 6:3 ff. states that the community presented seven men to the apostles; and they prayed and laid their hands on them, which was the usual ancient custom of imposing hands to symbolize the communication of a gift, blessing or authority (1 Tim. 4: 14, 5: 22). Two things are noteworthy for the text in Acts: First, the word "diakonia" occurs twice referring to the "service of distribution of food" and the "service of the word." Secondly, this concept of service among the people of God is very ancient. It filters back to Isaiah in the Suffering Servant Songs about the one who would give up his life for the people (Is. 50; 1-11; 52: 13-53; 1-12). Jesus is identified by the early church as the perfect Suffering Servant who lays down his life for His people (Heb. 5: 1-10). Ordained service in the early church is shared by the apostles and extended to St. Paul (Acts, 29: 19; Rom. 11:13; 1 Tim. 1: 12). In the very early days of the church community, the apostles recognized that even Judas who had shared, "this ministry of ours (of service and preaching), meant that they had to make a choice to select someone to take over the ministry and apostolic responsibility, which Judas had abandoned (Acts, 1:15). The concept of service (diakonia) is no less wonderfully expressed by St. Paul in, Acts, 21: 19, Romans, 11: 13, and in 1 Timothy, 1: 2. St. Paul identifies Timothy as his disciple and fellow co-worker, in this concept of service: "From Paul and Timothy, servant of Christ Jesus, to all the saints in Christ Jesus together with their bishops and Deacons." (Phil. 1: 1). This passage says something that is very interesting. Paul speaks of only two orders, the bishops and deacons. The priests in this text are apparently missing. It sounds strange, but evidently in the early church deacons were more recognized than priests. What is clear in this reading is that deacons held a distinct order of service closely associated with the chief leaders or overseers of the Christian communities.

Deacons were first described as men of service to distribute food to the people of God. It becomes clear that their service encompasses more than feeding people and waiting on tables. The deacon Philip preached and performed miracles which built great enthusiasm for the gospel in a Samaritan town (Acts, 8: 4-8). Stephen is singled out by the author of Acts, not only because he was filled with grace and power performing miracles with among the people, but also because he had wisdom from the Holy Spirit to preach and defend the gospel. It was his preaching that stirred up the people (Acts, 7: 1-10). Stephen was the first Christian martyr. When Stephen was stoned to death Saul (Paul) was present (Acts; 7: 60-8: 1). This event had a profound effect on Paul and set the stage for the churches reflection about the responsibilities and character of a bishop and deacon in 1 Tim. 3: 8-15.

"In the same way, deacons must be respectable men, whose word can be trusted, not addicted to much wine, not greedy for gain. They must be conscious believers in the mystery of the faith, Let them be tested first, and allowed to serve as deacons only after they have proved themselves blameless. Deacons must not have been married more than once; must be men who manage their children and their households well. Those who serve well as deacons will gain a high standing for themselves as well as winning a deep assurance in their efforts to promote faith in Christ Jesus." This passage shows us that the qualities necessary in bishops and deacons and that deacons must have a deep faith in the person of Jesus. Their confidence and sense of assurance comes from Christ. Their task of evangelizing was recognized

by their faithfulness to the people of God and to their missionary calling to serve.

Very early church documents inform us that the deacons were of great help to the bishops, so much so, that they could be called the eyes and ears of the bishop in the Christian community. Church witnesses portray the deacons as those who take care of the poor, and the sick. They show love for orphans and for the widowed. They bring the Holy Eucharist to those confined to their homes because of illness. They baptize, preach God's word, and join in other sacramental services. They are fervent in spirit, affirm all that is good, and serve all the people of God. Later church history reveals that deacons were given added responsibilities, such as serving as an official representative for the bishop, oversight in the day-to-day affairs of the local churches, serving as emissaries for the Pope and to kings and councils. The ministry of the deaconate was very important in the early church (Lumen gentium, 1965).

The permanent diaconate began to slowly disappear in the west and by the thirteenth century it was appropriated as a stepping stone to the priesthood. This corresponded to the rise of the monastic movement and the social changes in Europe. It is interesting to know that St. Francis of Assisi, was a deacon and did not aspire to the priesthood.

The Second Vatican Council, troubled by the shortage of workers in the Lord's vineyard, expressed the desire that the permanent diaconate be restored to an established position in the hierarchy. The council's document "of the Church," stated that the Order of Deacons could be conferred upon married men. Pope Paul VI commenting on the deaconate said, *"From the apostolic age the diaconate has had a clearly outstanding position among those ministries, and it has always been held in great honor by the church."* Pope Paul VI , on June 27th, 1967, promulgated the document authorizing the revival of the permanent diaconate in his Apostolic Letter, "Ad Pascendam,' on August 15th, 1972." He established the norms for the Order of Diaconate in this letter. He quotes passages from ancient Christian writers that make wonderful reading for everyone and especially for those interested in the permanent diaconate.

My ordination brought us many wonderful graces and experiences. A major thread began to emerge since our conversions in 1970, We felt a growing compassion and connection to the people of the "third world." Bea and I began to see and experience a pattern of God's activity in our lives and to trust Him to provide for us every day. We took to heart these words of Jesus in the scriptures:

"If you wish to be my disciple, sell what you have, give it to the poor (Matt, 19: 34), and demy yourself take up your cross and follow me."(Mk. 8: 34). The words of the bishop in my ordination echoed in my heart: *"Believe what you read, teach what you believe, and live what you teach."* Living a life of divine providence does not seem so difficult in a monastery but how can it be lived in a family with all the financial and social needs of a wife and six children? If it was just Bea and I on such an adventure, that would have been easy for us. Yet, it was as though our family had received an invitation from Jesus , *to be his disciple, sell all, and to give all.* Our children were part of God's providence too and Bea and I agreed that their needs and happiness came with financial requirements that we and God must account for and provide. Those expectations were important to us and to the Lord.

We were gently led by the Holy Spirit to live-out our trust in God's providence that His concerns and ours were the same. Even though our financial resources were being depleted as I served (twenty-four-seven) to the community of faith. The "hundredfold" of money was a startling experience of Divine provision but it was not a bottomless resource, like the jug and jar of the widow at Zarephath; nor could we find any ravens to bring us bread in the morning and meat in the evening (I Kings, 17:1-16). Still, we somehow fared well enough materially, through various donations and support provided by our Heavenly Father and his people. So, like St. Paul we learned say:

'It gave me great joy in the Lord that your concern for me bore fruit once more......I do not say this because I am in want, for whatever the situation I find myself in, I have learned to be self-sufficient. I am experienced in being brought low, yet I know what it is to have an abundance. I have learned to cope with every circumstance—how to eat well or go hungry, to be well provided for, or do without. In Him who is the source of my strength. I have strength for everything" (Phil, 4: 10 ff).

Bea and I were carried by the Father's invisible love and support. We received comfort from the source of all riches and goodness. We were blessed by the God who knows all and whose provision created all things. He never abandoned us whether in a season of plenty or in a season of need. We began to understand more deeply that earthly darkness is but the foreshadowing of heavenly light; that earthly trials can merely mask His closeness but not overcome it. We grasped ever more directly how "all things work together for the good of those who love God" (Rom. 8: 28). How every created thing, mountain and valley, evening shadow and ray of dawn, gives sublime evidence of God's loving providence (Psalm, 150).

Many of our friends and relatives thought that our decisions were not realistic or even understandable, and certainly not profitable. Paradoxically these judgements led us to a deeper appreciation of the cross of Jesus. It is the place where suffering purifies the spirit in preparation for our eternal joy. Our loving Father shows His care and concern just as wonderfully in sorrow and in gladness. God is the artist in our life who paints and reveals the portrait of the loving character of His Son living in us. *"We are God's work of art, created in Christ to live a life of goodness, according to his designs from the very beginning"* (Eph. 2: 10).

Contemplation of God's love and kindness led Bea and I to the conviction that holiness is for all and that everyone, not just priests and religious, are called to Christian perfection. Such contemplation guided us, in the Spirit, to a deeper love for the "church," the mystical body of Christ (I Cor. 12: 27). Jesus showed us what it meant to trust him even in the smallest things because, "He is the *way*, the *truth* and the *life*" (Jn. 14: 6). It is in faith that our Lord lives in our hearts in the Word, the Sacraments, and in the prayers of His people and calls us to follow him on the way.

If all Christians were really committed to follow Jesus, they would become, each in their own way, life, truth and the way to serve others which leads to a better world. Since they are the eyes, ears, hands and feet of Jesus, they would extend all over the earth His love for the poor, His compassion for the weak, His willingness to suffer for everyone no matter rich or poor. Humanity could launch out in new directions and become less polarized and enjoy the benefits of brighter days of joy and peace.

Beatrice and I learned that there were three things necessary for us to be faithful in our calling to minister to this broken world. The first thing was a spirit of poverty (Matt. 5: 2). This means living a simpler lifestyle and to be satisfied with what God provides. This contrasts the materialistic demands of culture and social standing that values the acquisition of more and more things. A willing spirit to share with others who are without is an essential Gospel mandate for God's blessing (Matt. 7: 7-12).

The second principle of ministry is the spirit of service. This means an overarching interest and concern for others, especially those in pain or trauma. The growing number of deacons worldwide is a wonderful sign that the spirit of service is not just a theological principle but is being lived out in a concrete way. St Paul puts it simply when he tells us in Philippians, "To consider everyone greater than themselves and to not be selfish" (Phil. 2: 3). Jesus also speaks of service and His willingness to meet our needs with his care (Jn. 13: 13-17). The ministry of service is throughout the Gospel because it is such a necessary part of following the Lord who came not to be served but to serve (Mk. 10: 45).

The third principle of ministry is to be led by the Holy Spirit. Let's face it! We cannot build ourselves up by trying to decipher with our human limitations God's plans without the Holy Spirit leading and guiding us. Holiness is how God sketches out His will for us through grace. It is through the Holy Spirit that any good is desired or accomplished according with His purposes. The answers to the problems of society, nations, families and ourselves resides in our attention to that small still voice that speaks healing and new life (Gal. 5: 25).

I offer you these three principles from the deepest conviction of my heart. They are the fruit of many experiences shared by me and my family. I have felt and understood, how relying on God to supply our needs leads to spiritual wealth; that suffering builds character which leads to a fuller life; that even frustration is often just a temporary holding pattern that leads to the fulfillment of God's plans. I feel blessed knowing that the spark of sacramental grace as a deacon can blaze up. The glory of this calling will overcome any pains of a dry heart in need of living water.

Endurance and perseverance point to something permanent. I attribute whatever I have gone through, hardships, trials, and struggles tied to the eminent grace of the permanent diaconate. Not only because it places within the soul the permanent marker of community service, but it is also like a fountain of blessings. It continually produces good desires, lasting resolutions, creativity, and adventure; all these being poured out in love from the Holy Spirit. I encourage anyone interested in this vocation to seek out information and to explore this unique gift to the church.

And that's not all!

CHAPTER VI

DEACON TRACTS

The guidance of the Holy Spirit is absolutely necessary to bring about Christ centered changes in the world and in ourselves. The gift of Leadership comes from the Holy Spirit. It is modeled after the twelve apostles, St. Paul, and the Deacons like St. Stephen who followed in the footsteps of the Lord. It is through a willing attention to the direction of the Holy Spirit on the part of the disciple that produces unwavering faith, trust and discernment of the Spirit's leading and direction. Believing in Jesus means deciding to be on a journey that is under the Lord's control. It requires that a person allows themselves to be led. This is not out of fear or a shallow kind of religious compliance but embraces the loving purposes of God's plan even when it is unclear to us (Hebrews, 12: 1-3). Our free consent is the response to God's perfect divine order. It is our "fiat" to the plans of a loving Father (Lk. 1: 35; Eph.1: 3-14). He does not demand our compliance. He invites our participation, that is the blessing, and with it comes our true identity and purpose. Being obedient to Him, who invites us into the wedding feast accepts the loving designs of our Creator (Matt. 22: 1-14) and our willingness to follow Him. By contrast, we see in the sin of Adam and Eve what willful disobedience produced, ignorance, miscommunication, suffering and death (Gen. 3: 16-42).

Mary, on the other hand, was happy to be the maid servant of the Lord. The fruit of her willing participation with God's plan of salvation produced the fruit in her womb of the long-promised King of her people and of us all. We are aware of the strife, hunger, sickness and poverty that the enemy has sown on the earth. Mary is the contrasting mirror of the Father's perfect plan of salvation in His Son. She is adorned with the first fruit of redemption like the bride (the church) coming to meet the bridegroom dressed in splendor and glory (Rev. 21: 1-10). We see in the Scriptures that The Son of Man comes like a shepherd who guides His flock by following His Father's will, becoming obedient to death on a cross so, *"There will be one flock and one shepherd. The reason why the Father loves Me is that I lay down my life, only to take it up again. Of my own free will I lay it down. And as it is in my power to lay it down, so it is in My power to take it up again. And this is the command I have received from My Father"* (John, 19: 16). Perfectly faithful to this command, Jesus allowed those who demanded His crucifixion and death to have their way. Even as sorrow and pain weigh heavily on His body and soul He sees beyond the suffering:

> *"Now sentence is being passed on this world; now the prince of this world*
> *Is to be overthrown. And when I am lifted up from the earth,*
> *I will draw all men to myself." (John, 12: 31).*

His ministry began by following the designs of the Father and the guidance of the Holy Spirit in His baptism (Matt. 3: 13-17). He was undeterred by the suffering He was to endure. He was obedient, far beyond the law's requirements, to the Father's purposes and His plan of Redemption that frees all of us from sin and death (Eph. 2: 14-22). We are also called to live in Jesus being obedient in following the Holy Spirit's leading and prompting. In St. Paul's letter to the Romans, 8: 14 it affirms us by saying, *"Everyone moved by the Spirit is a son of God."* This equates our sonship in the Holy Spirit to the gift of the divine Savior's suffering, death and resurrection as Son of God and son of man.

Without the guidance of the Holy Spirit, we are left to follow the advice of our own spirit, or the spirit of this world, or the spirit of fear and even the spirits of the enemy. Without the fruits of the Holy Spirit there is no way to evaluate the confused spirits of this age from the Father's work of grace. (Gal. 5: 13-23). It is so important for us to open our hearts without delay to the promptings of the Holy Spirit because the Holy Spirit produces good things and *"by their fruits we will know them"* (Matt, 7: 15-20). It is like comparing the taste of the wine at the wedding in Cana that the Lord produced that was so much better than the wine produced by the natural man (Jn. 2: 1-12). The Bridegroom adds the

Spirit of love, kindness, gentleness, the fruits of the Spirit to produce the best moral outcomes and the glorious vintage of eternal life. The positive effects of the activity of the Holy Spirit deepen our love for Jesus and the Father and the people of God in serving them.

The Holy Spirit of truth endows the believers with spiritual experiences (grace) in praise and worship, healing, prophetic word, teaching, correcting and revealing His loving purposes lived out in the community of faith (1 Cor 12: 1-12). This calling carries the Apostolic DNA of Pentecost through the Word, the Sacraments, Prayer and Catholic dogma and teaching. The scriptures say, *Eye has not seen , nor ear heard, and it has never entered the heart of man to envision what God has prepared for those who love Him"* (1 Cor, 2: 19-20). God also reveals the reflection of His love, power, beauty, goodness in the mosaic designs in the world of nature which can draw us to Him through contemplation of the wonders of creation. There is, however, a personal and intimate alliance between the Gospel, brought to us from the Father by His Son, and the ongoing illuminations of the Spirit given to us by the Father through Jesus. It should strengthen our bond to the love of the Blessed Trinity. Several scriptures from St. John's Gospel highlight this intimate connection to the church and to each one of us:

"I shall ask the Father. And He will give you another Advocate to remain with you forever. He is the Spirit of Truth. Whom the world could never receive, since He is with you—He is in you" (Jn. 14: 16-17). *...I have said these things to you, while I was still with you But the Advocate, the Holy Spirit, Whom the Father will send in my name, will teach you everything and remind you of everything that I have said to you"* (Jn. 14: 25-26).

"When the Advocate comes, whom I shall send to you from the Father, the Spirit of Truth, Who issues from the Father, He will be My witness." (Jn. 15: 26).

When the Spirit of Truth comes, He will lead you to the complete truth, since He will not be speaking as from Himself but will say only what He has learned (from the Father through Me); and will tell you of the things to come. Everything the Father has is mine; that is why I said: 'All He tells you will be taken from what is mine' (Jn. 15: 13-15).

From the union between Jesus and His Spirit flows another bond of love and that is the guidance and presence of the Holy Spirit in the Church. Much like a boat that needs the rudder and the wind to fill its sails and propel it forward, the church needs the breath of the Holy Spirit to power it in the direction of the Fathers purpose. Without the rudder to keep it on course, which is the teaching, the scriptures and doctrines of the Church, the boat would simply be blown off course. However, without the power of the Spirit it would just remain motionless in the doldrums of apathy and human control. Both elements are essential to steer and empower the vessel to move through the uncharted waters of each generations problems, and the challenges of preaching the Gospel. The Pentecostal Spirit is given to individuals in the same way it was given to the primitive church (Acts, 6: 5-7). The Apostles were guided by the awesome love of the Holy Spirit for efficacious preaching, teaching, in miracles and by sharing a common life together (Acts, 3: 1-10) We see the evidence of the Holy Spirit's presence in His miraculous gifts when we pray together with expectant faith, the Divine providence of hope and by living within the fellowship in the love of Jesus for the people of God.

St Paul does caution the community to a life of self-examination and to remain within the boundaries of Apostolic teaching and personal moral living (1 Gal. 5: 13-26). I have also drawn from the Spiritual Exercises of St. Ignatius, "the rules for discernment," as a tool to remain grounded within the guidance and direction of following where the Spirit leads (Loyola, 1999). Do not be reluctant to study the writings of St. Theresa of Avila, John of the Cross, Francis De Sales, Paul of the Cross and others. It is also an important part of spiritual growth to have a learned and experienced spiritual director.

The love that Bea and I have for the Holy Spirit has grown within the context of our love for each other, our family and the church. After all we are all parts of the Body of Christ (1 Cor. 12: 12-26). God will continue to pour out His graces and gifts upon us all as we move in tandem with His calling to serve His people. His glory is manifested in the gifts of the Holy Spirit like dew in the cool morning air even at this moment in time (2 Cor. 3: 12-19) So, we can move confidently in His glory.

And that's not all!

CHAPTER VII

DIVINE PROVIDENCE

I did not know that God was calling me and our family into a deeper walk of trust in Divine Providence. I was just becoming more attracted to a life of simplicity and the beauty of hands-on work. I had mastered the world of salesmanship, white collar management, and entrepreneurial business creation. I began to find peace and blessings in working with my hands as a carpenter, which was a skill I learned after my military service. Bea and I decided to simplify our life and to leave the hot desert of Phoenix and move to Prescott Arizona that had a more temperate climate where I could practice my craft and develop our ministry.

The city of Prescott's elevation is 5,300 feet and is largely a resort and tourist center. Its history dates back to the days of the US Calvary after the Civil War. It was a settlement for miners and cowboys. The early capital of the state of Arizona was Prescott. Its verdant landscapes, preserved by seasonal snow and sustained by a mild climate, is a restful slow-paced community for those needing to escape big city stresses and lifestyles. We moved the family to Prescott in September 1972 after my ordination in May.

It was not easy, at that time, to find a house for us. There was very little available on the market, which included even rental properties. I spent all day with Jim Thomas who lived there and was also a real estate agent and was in the Deacon program with me. He presented me with a possible solution. He and his partner had a house that was unfinished but nearly completed. Bea and I went out to see it. The house fit exactly what we needed, so we struck an agreement by which I would finish the family room and two bedrooms downstairs and apply the cost of my labor and materials toward the rent. In a couple of weeks, we were able to move in. It did not take long for us to become acquainted with several people in the Assumption Prayer Group and the new Catholic church we attended. I began working with the sick and elderly in the parish.

Sometimes God places something in your heart through a personal experience. In my hospital ministry I saw a growing number of patients that were sick because of drug and alcohol abuse. I recall a meeting that was held at the diocesan office. All my fellow Deacons were there and after the gathering was over, I was in the parking lot saying goodbye. Just then a man approached me, who was very intoxicated and just fell into my arms, as if he was looking for me to hold him up. I felt a wave of compassion wash over me. We were able to help him, but it was clear that he needed treatment and care. That seed of God's mercy for the broken-hearted was planted in my heart at that moment and it has never left me. In the course of my ministry, I became aware of the need for a place to care for this part of Christ's Body. My family was supportive and willing to participate it this calling. It seemed, at first blush, to be risky, difficult and painful. I strongly felt that something must be done. I began praying for the Holy Spirit to provide a mission to help and support those on the journey to sobriety and healing. I prayed for a door to open to build such a place for alcohol and drug recovery.

This chapter and the next trace some of my ministry in Prescott and later to the world. It blossomed from early stage of trusting in God's Providence. This calling would extend later into bringing the Deaconate to Canada and an evangelism ministry which grew from the lessons Bea, and I learned in Prescott. Some people may judge us as foolish or overly naïve. We started something that we eventually walked away from. It looked to others as a failure, but to us, the journey of obedience to God's Spirit was its own reward and a training ground for our later ministry.

One day I was visiting with my good friend and fellow Deacon Jim Thomas, and we decided to take a drive over to some property that was available in my price range. It was a plain piece of property with little bushes and grassy rangeland with lots of volcanic rocks. It had a wonderful view overlooking a Willow lake with beautiful granite boulders on the north side. It was quiet and serene. The dam was built to hold the seasonal water from rains and snow.

It was unimproved land that rose slightly above the road with a flat mesa on the southern edge of the property. It was a 10-acre parcel. I felt instantly that this was the place that God had in mind to build our healing center. I had some money from the sales of my companies, and I bought it. The idea was to make it the site of a Charismatic Center for Healing of Addicted Persons. I felt confident that if God would provide the necessary resources (materials and equipment) to accomplish the task of building Montserrat. I picked this name after a famous monastery and a center of Marion piety in Spain. I began to start working on the project. Under the great expanse of cobalt blue sky, alone with my thoughts and prayers, I could hear what the Lord desired. *"You are right in hearing I wanted you to work with your hands. Now I would have you work with your hands for Me and Me alone."*

My vision for the center began to grow as I began a daily routine of working on the property. It was to be a community of deeply committed individuals and families coming together for the purpose of reaching out in a healing ministry, principally but not exclusively for alcoholics. Even now as I look back on those days, I can still imagine the staff assembling together; people of science, with spiritual wisdom—monks perhaps, priests and sisters and married couples their families and single people whose lives are devoted to the service of caring for the body of Christ. It would include psychiatrists, counselors, social workers, and teachers working with a common purpose to help restore the afflicted patient and their family to physical, emotional and spiritual health and recovery.

Ongoing education and spiritual growth would be an essential part of the staff's commitment to care. The program would include residents and interns who would donate their time to be trained through this ministry to extend this work beyond Montserrat into their own practice.

The ministry would also include inner-healing, and life skills training for the patients and their families. There would also be daily and weekly groups for those receiving in-patient treatment and for those needing out-patient support. There would be after discharge job placement through community business connections and working with our social work staff for out-patient housing and for other resources if needed. Montserrat's model was radical for its time in 1973-1976. Many of these concepts and ideas have been integrated and developed by other programs since then and now exist for drug and alcohol treatment and recovery.

Growth in the spiritual life was indispensable in the Montserrat model that began to emerge through prayer, work, and struggle. The importance of personal conversion to Christ and service to the community are anchors for healing and recovery. Participation is liturgical worship, personal prayer, along with spiritual mentors will support the patient and their families adjustments to a sober way of life and strengthen the bonds of caring within the family. When the patient returns home there will be a counselor to help them make changes and support the families reintegration and healing. This model is based spiritually on the Ignatian Exercises as foundational principles of sober living with sober values and community support.

The Montserrat project was only a small part of many ideas for ministry that are still being created today by Deacons all over the world. They dream of new missions and solutions to the world's brokenness. They see themselves as partners of Jesus in the Holy Spirit, glorifying the work of the Father's hands. The numbers of Deacons continues to multiply worldwide and with it comes more outlets for service to the people of God, and a growing witness to God's transforming love in the world.

"In the days to come—it is the Lord who speaks—I will pour out my spirit on all mankind. Their sons and daughters shall prophesy, your young men shall see visions, your old men shall dream dreams" (Acts, 2: 17-21).

This was my dream that I still carry with me to this day, because God's Word always bears fruit.

And that's not all!

CHAPTER VIII

MISSIONARIES

The authentic inspiration of the Holy Spirit leads to an increasing commitment to the service of Jesus Christ. The signs and wonders that follow the genuine preaching of the Word initiates in us an eagerness to respond by following the Lord in any circumstance that we may face. The cost of this invitation becomes less of a concern to the Disciple as they grow in faith, hope and love. Through difficulties and in times of perseverance born out of suffering, belief moves the person into action (Bonhoffer, 1963). It can be said that we believe only to the extent that it causes us to act (James, 2: 14-26). Trusting in the Word of God places us at the doorstep of His mercy and love. Bea and I and our family divested ourselves of worldly possessions voluntarily to live in the precious Kingdom offered to everyone by Jesus. It is important to be filled with the Holy Spirit, led by the Holy Spirit and obey the Holy Spirit. Jesus invites us, through the course of events, to choose His pattern of life not the pattern of control and the manipulation of events for our advantage. If Jesus is the Lord, He must be the Lord of every area of our lives, even our material existence (Mk. 10: 17-31). This does not mean a life of inactivity, on the contrary, the pattern of life we receive in Jesus becomes filled with the new found joy of his activity as He reveals the kingdom of His grace to us (Phil. 4: 4-7). This new life keeps us very close and dependent on His divine providence. Jesus delights in surprising us as He showers us with consolations that our minds, cluttered with fear, anxiety and self-interest, cannot begin to grasp.

Our second trip to Rome was a surprise. We were living in a mobile home in Prescott Valley and were praying about moving. We did not know where or when, but we felt the Lord had other plans for our ministry. We received a call from Father Paul who had moved to Canada, that friends of his were coming to Arizona. He asked if I would meet them in Phoenix to show them around the valley. I met them in the lobby of their hotel a few days later. They were all Charismatic Catholics. We rejoiced in the Lord as we shared our experiences living in the Holy Spirit. Our new brothers and sisters were God's gift to us that day. The wife of one of the men suggested to her husband that night that the Lord was leading her to ask if they might forgo a trip they planned to Hawaii and instead send Bea and I to Rome for the International Charismatic Conference They decided to ask us the next day if we would be willing for them to send us. We were astonished by their unselfishness and the power of the Holy Spirit. There were only ten days left before the conference. We had not even given ourselves permission to even think about going since we had no money, and accommodations would be expensive and difficult to obtain. There would be many pilgrims in Rome because there was also a Holy Year celebration planned. They asked if we would go with them to California for a few days. We spent a joyous time of spiritual dialogue and prayer as we toured California ending up in San Diago. It was like a personalized retreat. They went on to San Francisco and we returned to Prescott Valley. They arranged every detail to make our trip worry free, even supporting the cost of child care while we were gone. We met them back in San Francisco the day before we left on our second trip to Rome.

A pilgrimage is expected to provide some inconvenience to the pilgrim. This was also true for me. When we arrived in Rome, we found our lodgings were located forty miles from the Vatican on the Mediterranean Sea. My wife and I were to share a kitchen of a three-bedroom apartment in an unfinished apartment house. The three bedrooms were inhabited by nine women. It's a good thing that I had so many sisters in my family growing up. Bea and I managed the situation somehow as best we could. I was truly blessed among women. It would have been nice to have a private rose covered villa, but God's grace made up for our inconvenience in so many ways.

We met so many friends in the Lord from all over the world. It seemed more like a big family reunion. Jesus took us from glory to glory. We were present in St. Peter's on Pentecost and the following day. I was able to assist at Mass as a Deacon from the Pope's altar. I remember very vividly saying to the priest next to me as we stepped up to the altar, "I really feel married, this cincture I am wearing is very tight because it is a belt from one of my wife's suits." I had forgotten mine.

I will never forget the half hour of prayer we had in the Chapel of the Holy Eucharist before processing down to the main altar. The sound of the praise and worship of 750 Priests, Deacons, Bishops and Cardinals from all over the world, singing in tongues will live in my heart forever. It was at this Mass that our Holy Father proclaimed his approval of the Charismatic movement in the Catholic Church and that it was an authentic gift of the Holy Spirit (Pope Paul VI, Ecclesiam Suam, 1964).

The conference itself was another grace-filled blessing of God's mercy and love. It was held on the grounds above the catacombs. There was such a sense of union with those early Christians who suffered so much because they truly loved Jesus. We could feel the blessing of the Communion of the Saints. The Joy of the Holy Spirit was all around us. We attended the healing seminar that Father Francis McNutt conducted. Father Paul was there, and he asked my wife and I to minister healing to the French speaking brothers and sisters who needed prayer. We prayed over people in French for almost two hours and saw the glory of God as He answered our prayers on the spot. The joy of the experience prompted me to say as I laughed, "I think God must be French!"

Another experience of how God answers the secret desires of our heart was revealed to us after the Charismatic Conference was over. We had only three days left of our stay near Rome. We were looking for the residence of the Marist Fathers to find a priest we had met at the conference. Our cab driver knew the approximate location but after seeing some of the same side streets for several times we decided to call their residence for directions. When I called, I dialed the wrong number. I had called the Sisters of the Holy Family of Bordeaux by mistake. Three years before out trip to Rome, we had a sister from this order stay with our family. She learned about our ministry from Fr. Paul in Canada. She was thirty-five years old and had spent the last twelve years in a wheelchair as a result of crippling arthritis. She came to live with us in our home for the climate and treatment at a local arthritis center. She brought another sister with her who was a nurse and a member of her order. While they were with us, they received the baptism of the Holy Spirit. She also had surgery on her knee, hip and toes. They stayed with us for four months. They were wonderful sisters in the Lord and loved them very dearly. They had asked us to be sure to call their Mother House if we were ever in Rome. The sister who answered the phone gave us direction to the convent, which was nearby, and invited us to lunch. We changed our plans and went to meet these sisters, most of whom we had never met. They were very hospitable and gracious. They insisted we spend the next three days with them. I went with one of the sisters and returned to pick-up our luggage from where we had been staying. When I returned to the Mother House, they showed us our quarters. It was on the edge of their property and was the most beautiful little villa surrounded by roses. It was to be our home for the next three days. When we moved in Bea and I were praising God for our own bedroom and our own bath, study and living room.

All that we desired had been given to us. While we were praising God there was one more thing that came to my mind. *"Oh, Father there's only one thing lacking, how I'd like a good cigar."*

It was a custom that when there was a special occasion for celebration, especially when Michael came to visit us from the seminary that we each have a cigar. We would take the day off and spend it together with the Lord Jesus. We would talk about what our experiences of the Holy Spirit and witness and share together the love of God in our lives. I had been trying to buy one cigar since our arrival in Rome but to no avail. I had to write a brief report, and I had nothing down on paper. Bea called by attention to a big carved desk in the study with a large inviting chair. I sat down in the chair and began exploring the desk for paper and writing instruments. Everything I needed was there. How surprised and blessed I was when I opened the top drawer and found three boxes of Havana cigars. How they found their way into the desk of a study in a villa in a convent is no small miracle in itself. We blessed God for being so mindful of us.

Many other memories fill my heart as I look back and reflect on what the Lord showed us on this trip. They are too numerous to mention. Lives lived for the glory of God continually touch, strengthen and transmit faith. The saints of tomorrow are already alive today. We leave an imprint on future lives by planting these seeds of faith. As we are led by the Holy Spirit, we witness the beauty of our lives reflecting the beauty of the Lord (Tim.2: 1-8).

And that's not all!

FINAL THOUGHTS

Every person's life contains elements of polarities, highs-lows, agony-ecstasy, sin-redemption, life-death. These opposites can be as a result of our own doing. They can be the effect of our personal relationships, social and economic struggles, or just the realities of our human nature (Savage, 2016). They can also be as a result to following the leading and prompting of the Holy Spirit. How we decide to respond to these polarities is our choice. Living in the Holy Spirit means that we take on the character of Jesus with life's joys and sorrows, successes and failures. We see these themes in the Suffering Servant Songs of the Prophet Isaiah that parallel the life and death and resurrection of Jesus our precious savior (Is. 42: 1-9; 41:1-6; 50: 4-9; 52: 13-15; 53: 1-12). Jesus calls us as sons and daughters and heirs to the kingdom. Did we not drink of the same Spirit? The authentic servant of God will respond gratefully to St. Paul's answer to Job for the reason for suffering. *In my flesh I make up for what is lacking in Christ's trials, for the sake of His Body, which is the Church*" (Col. 1: 24). And also *"The sufferings of this present time cannot be compared with the glory that is to be revealed in us.*"(Rom. 6: 18).

One of our greatest difficulties is knowing what to keep and what to give away. What we don't understand also produces fear. What we cannot control about our lives, or the lives of others produces feelings of powerlessness and fear. Perhaps our greatest fear is of being alone. It is so natural for us to seek human approval or belonging instead of the kind of the spiritual meaning and belonging that comes from God. *"How can you believe, since you look to one another for approval and are not concerned with the approval that comes from God?* (Jn. 5: 44). It is precisely when we come to Jesus alone do, we find Him ever near.

In my previous chapters I described only a few of the experiences and consolations given to us by Jesus. We were not exempt from times of desolation too. The call to a comprehensive conversion is a radical call and the answer to the call is a radical answer. It is a turning around that requires a willingness to embrace the teachings of Christ and His Church. This call often brings the disciple into conflict with the way the world operates. The persecutions we have suffered for following the leading of the Holy Spirit into divine providence are numerous. The Beatitudes (Matt: 5: 1-12) illustrate the nature of these hardships. They begin with the poor receiving the Kingdom of Heaven and end with the persecuted receiving the same Kingdom. It has been our experience that if we make ourselves poor, we will touch all the Beatitudes as the Holy Spirit leads us. Listen to the words in Mark's Gospel (Mk. 8: 34-38).

"He called the people and his disciples to him and said 'If anyone wants to be a follower of mine, let him renounce himself and take up the cross and follow me. For anyone who wants to save his life will lose it; but anyone who loses his life for my sake, and for the sake of the gospel, will save it. What gain, then, is it for a man to win the whole world and ruin his life? And indeed, what can a man offer in exchange for his life? For if anyone in this adulterous and sinful generation is ashamed of me and of my words the Son of Man will also be ashamed of him when he comes in the glory of his Father with the angels."

The kingdom of Jesus requires our recognition and consent to enter into and receive this pure gift of salvation "now' with our whole heart.

Praise the Lord!

And that's not all!

BIBLIOGRAPHY

Bible, *The Jerusalem Bible, Readers Edition (JB)*, (1966). New York, NY., Doubleday

Bible, *The New American Bible, Revised Edition, (NAB)* (2008) Charlotte, NC, St. Benedict Press

Bible, *The New International Version, (NIV)*, (2011) Grand Rapids, MI, Zondervan

Bonhoffer, D., (1063). *The Cost of Discipleship*, New York, NY., Scribner Book Co.

Frost R., (2017). *Selected Poems of Robert Frost, Illustrated Edition*, New York, NY. Fall River Press

French, R. M., (2012). *The Way of the Pilgram; and the Pilgram Continues His Way*, Baldwin Greens, London, England, SPCK Publishing

John of the Cross, (1991). *The Collected Works of St. John of the Cross*, Washington, DC., ICS Publications

Loyola, I, (1999). *The Spiritual Exercises of St. Ignatius at Manresa*, Charlotte, NC., TAN Books

National Bulletin on the Liturgy, Vol. 3, (1969). *Catholic Rite of Ordination of a Deacon*

Paul V1, (1972). *Ad Pascendam*, Dicastero per la Comunicazone, Liberia Edtrice Vaticana

Paul, VI, (1964). *Ecclesiam Suam*, Dicastero per la Comunicazone, Liberia Edtrice Vaticana

Paul, V1, (1967). *Sacrum Diaconatus Ordinem*, Dicastero per la Comunicazone Liberia Edrice Vaticana

Pokrovsky, G, (2001*). The Way of the Pilgram, The Jesus Prayer Journey*, Woodstock, VA., Skylight Paths

Roer, P., (2012). *St. Ignatius of Antioch; the Epistles*, Create Space Independent Publishing Platform

Savage, J., (1996*). Listening & Caring Skills, A Guide for Groups and Leaders*, Nashville, TN. Abingdon Press

St. Agustine 272, https//www.earlychurchtexts.com/public/Augustine_sermon_272eucharist.html

Teresa of Avila, (1980). *The Collected Works of St. Teresa of Avila, Revised Edition, Vol. 1,* Washington, DC., ICS Publications

Vatican II, Council, dogm.Const.ontheChurch,lumengentiumn.21: AAS 57,25,and 36

ACKNOWLEDGEMENTS

Special thanks to Fr. Brice Zurmuehlem (now with the Lord) who worked with Deacon Joe and wrote down the first draft of this autobiography of his life and early ministry. To the family, Michael, Susan, Barbara, Richard, and the rest of the family along with their children, thank you.

I have also greatly benefited from the support and help of Ms. Karen Myers.

Although Deacon Joe has joined Fr. Brice and his Wife Bea in heaven his lasting impact on the church and the lives, he touched will always celebrate his calling and the love, adventure and joy in living in the grace of the Holy Spirit.

Editor, Ezra Small + 2024 Fr. and Brice Zurmuehlem CP

Ms. Karen Meyer

"And that's not all" is a book that has been waiting for years to be released. This book is the true events of Deacon Joseph Lessard's awakening to the power of the Holy Spirit in his life and the impact it left on him and this world. If you are open to being uplifted, challenged, and strengthened in believing in the Power of God, I encourage you to enjoy this book. It is written as if you are listening to Deacon Joe relate to you personally his experiences of God's providential love and the unexpected wonder of that love in his life.

The editor took up a difficult challenge to write this book in his dad's words. I appreciate his including personal insights and biblical reflections of how the Holy Spirit was making Deacon Joe aware of the connections with the "Living Word" in his own life experiences. His openness to being led by the Holy Spirit is an adventure!

I recommend you enjoy the witness of someone who not only preached the Word but lived it. I remember asking Joe once, "What do you say to a person who doesn't believe in God?" His response "Tell them a miracle." Then

I said, "and if they still don't believe?" "Tell them another miracle!' I imagine that's why his book is titled, "And that's not all"!

Deacon Joe Lessard - A Legend
Deacon Joe Lessard was an icon as a Roman Catholic Deacon in
Phoenix and in Canada. I had the privilege and joy of meeting
him and enjoying his friendship during my diaconal training and
following my own ordination in 2002 as a Deacon in Phoenix, AZ.
I experienced firsthand his holiness and love of the Holy Spirit as
he and his wife evangelized throughout the United State and
Canada. I saw the results of his healing ministry. I look forward
to rejoicing with him as we both rest in the hands of our Lord.
Deacon Lou Cornille
Permanent Deacon, Diocese of Phoenix

Dale Maingot

Every so often, we are truly blessed to have our lives touched and profoundly impacted by the life of a soul especially graced by God and placed into the realm of our lives for the sole purpose of drawing us closer to God. Deacon Joseph Lessard was one of those people for me. From the first time I met Joe and his wife, Beatrice, forty years ago I sensed that our lives would become intertwined in ways I couldn't begin to imagine at the time.

Initially attending Joe's Bible seminars in Alberta, Canada, where he shared many of the stories and experiences found between the pages of this book, to formation as a Spiritual Companion under his direction, I came to know and love Joe and Bea deeply. I was most blessed, however, to have Joe as my spiritual director and mentor; indeed, my journey in faith – especially lessons learned about surrender to the will of God's divine providence - is a direct testament to his guidance and tutelage.

This poignant autobiography is the story of a life well-lived, a life based on complete surrender to the One who had His hand upon Joe from childhood, and who led him to a life of total surrender and service. May it inspire you the way Joe inspired me and if you have never done so, cause you to seek God's holy will for your life.

www.ingramcontent.com/pod-product-compliance
Lightning Source LLC
Chambersburg PA
CBHW031232120626
46545CB00003B/1093